OXFORD
Illustrated
Computer
Dictionary

Written and illustrated by
Ian Dicks

Edited by
Andrew Solway

OXFORD
UNIVERSITY PRESS

Great Clarendon Street, Oxford OX2 6DP

Oxford University Press is a department of the University of Oxford.
It furthers the University's objective of excellence in research,
scholarship, and education by publishing worldwide in

Oxford   New York

Auckland   Cape Town   Dar es Salaam   Hong Kong   Karachi
Kuala Lumpur   Madrid   Melbourne   Mexico City   Nairobi
New Delhi   Shanghai   Taipei   Toronto

With offices in

Argentina   Austria   Brazil   Chile   Czech Republic   France   Greece
Guatemala   Hungary   Italy   Japan   Poland   Portugal   Singapore
South Korea   Switzerland   Thailand   Turkey   Ukraine   Vietnam

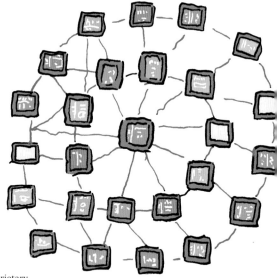

Oxford is a registered trade mark of Oxford University Press
in the UK and in certain other countries

© Ian Dicks 2006

The moral rights of the author have been asserted

Database right Oxford University Press (maker)

First published 2006

British Library Cataloguing in Publication Data

Data available

hardback
ISBN-13: 978-0-19-911241-8
ISBN-10: 0-19-911241-X

paperback
ISBN-13: 978-0-19-911240-1
ISBN-10: 0-19-911240-1

10 9 8 7 6 5 4 3 2 1

Printed in Singapore

Contents

You can use this dictionary to help you find any word connected to computers. It is organised by themes - from Computer basics, Hardware, Software, ICT and the Internet to Multimedia and Computer Jargon. If you think of a word and have an idea which of these themes it falls into, then go to the section and you will find the entries in alphabetical order there. If you have no idea where to start, try the alphabetical index on P103.

ICT is a big subject so, to help you build up a lot of knowledge, many entries have cross references to other related words. Use the cross references to skim through the book getting all the information you need.

There are also special feature pages that focus on the key ICT themes such as history or hardware.

fragmentation

Fragmentation is the way that related pieces of information become separated and scattered across a computer's hard disk. This happens slowly as more information is added to the disk. Eventually, this fragmentation slows the computer down. When this happens, you have to 'defragment' (tidy up) the disk.

➷ defragment p53

hang

When a computer hangs, it suddenly stops what it is doing and waits. Sometimes it is waiting for more information. Sometimes it carries on waiting for ever – in which case it is time to turn off and start again.

hang

import

To import data is to open files or information created in one program in a different program.

inactive window

The inactive window is any window other than the one you are using. Inactive windows appear behind the active window.

interface

An interface is a place where you and the computer communicate.
* Your keyboard is an interface where you can communicate by typing.
* Your mouse is another interface. You move the mouse and click it to communicate with the computer.
* Your monitor is an interface where the computer communicates with you.

*➷ keyboard p18 • mouse p9
monitor p19*

interfaces

initialize

To initialize a program is to start it up.

➷ program p30

headword in colour

clear and accurate definition

cross reference to other headword entries

theme

Do you know your analogue from your digital? Or your microchip from your motherboard? This first section has a feature page about the basics of computers. You can learn about programming a computer, the different types of computer, and what computers might be like in the future. There is also a feature page about the history of computers. Did you know that the first computers were bigger than a room, but slower than a modern laptop? There are also entries explaining some of the basic bits at the heart of a computer, and entries about some of the units that are used in computing.

programming a computer
to follow instructions

analogue signals

Analogue signals are a way of storing or sending information. When you talk into a telephone, for instance, the sound of your voice is turned into changing patterns of electricity that travel along the telephone wires. These patterns are an analogue signal. Analogue signals change smoothly. This is different from a digital signal, which is made up of a string of numbers. For a computer to understand analogue information, the analogue signals have to be converted to digital information.

digital p10

binary numbers

Binary numbers are a way of counting using only the numbers 1 and 0. Counting in binary goes like this: 'one, ten, eleven, a hundred, a hundred and one, a hundred and ten...' You can see the binary numbers for the first ten normal numbers in the table below. Computers store information and do calculations using binary numbers.

binary numbers	normal numbers
1	1
10	2
11	3
100	4
101	5
110	6
111	7
1000	8
1001	9
1011	10

bit

Bit is short for binary digit. A bit is the smallest piece of information your computer can handle. It takes eight bits of information to produce just one letter of the alphabet.

binary numbers p3

Boolean logic

Boolean logic is a set of rules used by computers, based on the use of simple 'true or false' questions. It is used by Internet search engines to gather information.

Internet p33

bus

A bus is a set of connections used by a computer's CPU (its 'brain') to communicate with other parts of the computer.

CPU p10

byte (b)

A byte is a way of measuring the amount of information a computer can handle. It is equal to eight bits, which is the information used to create or store a single letter. Most computers can store at least 30 million bytes (30 megabytes).

binary numbers

$1+1=10$

bit p3
megabyte p12

A computer is a machine that can do lots of different jobs. Most machines are designed to do only a few things. But a computer can do lots of different jobs because it can be programmed.

Following instructions

When you program a computer, you give it a set of instructions telling it how to do something. This could be anything from solving a difficult maths problem to drawing cartoon characters for an animated movie. The computer carries out the instructions much faster than a human could do, and without making mistakes. Computers are so useful that you can find them everywhere. People use computers at home and at work. Computers control machines that make everything from aircraft to pens. And there are even small computers in everyday machines like cars and radios.

programming a computer

Computers have not always been so important. In 1947 an expert thought that eighteen computers would be enough for the whole of the United States! Today there are over 400 million computers in the USA, and over a billion worldwide.

desktop

laptop

palmtop

the three tops

All shapes and sizes

Computers come in all shapes and sizes. The type we are most familiar with is the PC, or personal computer, that sits on our desks. Then there is the laptop, the size of a small briefcase and easy to carry around.

Even smaller than this is the PDA or personal digital assistant. This is the size of a notepad, and fits in your pocket.

Other computers can be very large. A mainframe computer is one that hundreds or thousands of people can use at the same time. Supercomputers are very fast: they can carry out hundreds of millions of instructions in a second.

Future computers

Computers are getting more and more powerful all the time. Scientists are always looking at new ways of improving computers. This usually means making them faster. One new idea that scientists are working on is the quantum computer. Most of today's computers carry out instructions one after the other, but a quantum computer could do lots of calculations at the same time. It would work billions of times faster than an ordinary computer.

an intelligent computer

Scientists are also developing wearable computers. These could be part of your clothing, or worn on your wrist like a watch. Another new kind of computer is one that can be rolled up like a piece of paper. You will be able to read it like a book or magazine. When you have finished with it you can simply roll it up and slip it in your pocket, or maybe use it to swat a fly…

the latest computer fashion

Microscopic computers

Perhaps the most interesting development of all could be the nanocomputer. This is a microscopically tiny computer just a few atoms across. Nanocomputers would be able to do all kinds of incredible things. Microscopic robots controlled by nanocomputers could do repairs inside your body.

Some scientists even imagine that nanocomputers could be grouped together to become nanocreatures. These would be tiny machines, more intelligent than human beings, that would be able to change their shape.

laptop p18
PC p20
program p26

5

● Computer games

There are thousands of different games that you can play on a computer. Some are computer versions of other kinds of games, such as chess or card games. Others are designed specially for computers. Computer games were originally very simple, because early computers could not cope with complicated graphics and sounds. The best known early computer game was called Space Invaders. You had to shoot down alien spaceships as they tried to land on Earth.

Different types of game

Today there are four main types of game. Strategy games are ones where you have to plan and think carefully about how to win - for instance games with battling armies. In adventure games you have to solve riddles and sometimes collect treasure or weapons as you follow a quest. Simulation games copy real life as closely as possible, for instance games where you fly a plane or drive a racing car. Action games range from straight fights to car chases.

Space Invaders

Some computers are specially designed just for playing computer games. They have extra-sharp graphics to make the games as realistic as possible. You can play many computer games by yourself. But with some games you can connect up with other computers through the Internet or another network, and play against your friends.

graphics p71
Internet p33
network p44

computer graphics have improved since the 1980's

© 2006 SEGA Corporation

© 2006 SEGA Corporation

adventure game

© 2006 SEGA Corporation

7

Computers have been around a lot longer than you think. About 2000 years ago the Babylonians invented the abacus. It was a hand calculator that used rows of beads sliding along wires in a wooden frame. The abacus is still used in many parts of the world today.

a Roman computer?

Calculators and punched cards

There were no new ideas in computing for about 1600 years after this. Then in 1623 a German scientist called Wilhelm Schickard built a machine called a Calculating Clock. It could quickly add and subtract six-figure numbers. This was probably the first ever calculator.

Over the next 200 years people came up with quite a few different mechanical calculators. But they all did only simple sums. Then in 1820 Charles Babbage designed a machine called the Difference Engine, which could do much more complex calculations. Unfortunately the machine was so complicated that only a small part of it was ever built. Charles went on to design an even more complicated machine called the Analytical Engine. It was never built, which is a pity, because it would have been the first ever programmable computer.

The first real computers

In the 1940s the first machines similar to our idea of a computer were built. These early computers were not laptops. One of them, a machine called ENIAC, weighed 30 tonnes! It used so much power that it caused an electricity shortage.

The early computers worked using large glass valves, which looked like thin light bulbs. Then in 1948 transistors were invented. These were much smaller than valves, and did not break so easily. Computers quickly got smaller and much faster.

One of the first computers you could actually buy was called the Univac. The first Univacs were made in the USA in 1951. They weighed over 12 tonnes and cost $159,000. Only the government and very large businesses could afford to buy computers like this.

The third generation

In 1959 a new invention marked the beginning of the modern computer. This was the microchip, which crammed hundreds of transistors and other electronic bits on to a silicon chip the size of a thumbnail.

Microchips made it possible to build the first home computers. They were called minicomputers. The first ones appeared in 1962. They cost £2000 and were not actually very small – about the size of a filing cabinet!

Early computers only had a keyboard to communicate with. Then in 1964 the first computer mouse was made. The next important developments were in the operating systems for personal computers – the programs that tell the computer what to do. The most famous of these were the DOS operating system, developed by Microsoft in 1982, and the Macintosh operating system developed by Apple in 1984. Today most of us use one or other of these systems on our computers.

the first ever microchip

computers of the future

What next?

In 1943 the chairman of the computer firm IBM predicted that the world would need maybe five computers. He couldn't have been more wrong. Today there are over a billion computers worldwide. Life has become almost unthinkable without them. They are used for playing games, for controlling space missions, and for everything in between. Who knows what else they will be used for in the future?

DOS p28
keyboard p18
Macintosh p19
operating system p30
program p30

calculate

To calculate is to work out by mathematical means. Another word for calculate is 'compute', hence the word computer.

central processing unit

This another way of saying CPU.

chip

This is another word for microchip.

microchip p12

chip

CPU (central processing unit)

The CPU is the 'brains' of a computer. It is made up of one or more small microprocessors (powerful microchips). The CPU carries out the millions of calculations that a computer does each second.

microchip p12

digital

Digital means 'using numbers'. A computer stores information, does calculations and communicates with other computers using long strings of binary numbers. Any information that you want to put into a computer, including pictures, music or movies, has to be digital. Otherwise the computer cannot understand it.

drive

A drive is a place on a computer where you can store information. The computer gives each of these drives a letter. Most computers have a hard disk. This is usually the C drive. There is usually also a slot or tray where you can put in CDs or DVDs and this is another drive. Some computers have more than one CD drive, or they may have a slot for a floppy disk. And you can attach all kinds of other storage devices to the computer, each of which becomes a separate drive.

**CD p16 • DVD p17
floppy disk p17 • hard disk p18**

formula

Formulas are often used in spreadsheets or databases. You can use a formula, for instance to multiply together two bits of number information, or to add up a list of numbers.

database p80 • spreadsheet p81

gigabyte (Gb)

A gigabyte is a measurement of the amount of information a computer can store. A gigabyte is a billion bytes, or 1000 megabytes. Some modern computers can store over 120 gigabytes of information. How many bytes is that?

byte p3 • megabyte p12

gigahertz (Ghz)

Gigahertz is a way of measuring the speed of a microprocessor.

input

Input is a word for any information fed into a computer.

interactive

An interactive program is one where the person using it has to answer questions or do things. Computer games and educational programs are good examples of interactive programs.

Kbps (kilobytes per second)

This is a measurement of how fast data is transferred. For instance, the fastest that you can download something from the Internet using a dial-up connection is about 56 Kbps.

data p80 • Internet p33 •
kilobyte p11

kilobyte

A kilobyte is a unit for measuring the amount of information a computer can handle. One kilobyte is just over a thousand bytes.

byte p3

Mbps (megabytes per second)

This is a measurement of how fast information can be sent and received. Broadband Internet connections are sometimes 1 or 2 Mbps.

broadband p37
byte p3
megabyte p12

Kbps

microchip

A microchip is a square of silicon about the size of a large postage stamp. The surface of the microchip is covered with very tiny electronic circuits. These are the 'brains' that make the computer work. Before microchips were invented, computers were much bigger and were less powerful.

computer history p8-9

megabyte (MB)

A megabyte is a measurement of how much information a computer can store, send, or receive. One byte is the information needed for a single letter. A megabyte is a million bytes.

byte p3

megabyte

megahertz (Mhz)

Megahertz is a measurement of the speed at which a computer can handle data (information). The higher the computer's speed, the faster the programs work.

data p80 • program p30

motherboard

The motherboard is the main circuit board of a computer. It includes the central processing unit.

CPU p10 • circuit board p16

output

The output from a computer is any information coming out of it, for instance through the printer, through the speakers or on the monitor.

monitor p19 • printer p21

Hardware

This section is all about hardware - the bits and pieces of machinery that make up a computer. The first article tells you about the 'brains' of the computer, and about different kinds of peripherals. There's also something about the different types of memory a computer has. The other entries will help you to sort out all the different kinds of computer. You can learn the difference between a Mac and a PC, and know your laptop from your palmtop. You can find out about different kinds of data storage, such as hard disks, CDs, and DVDs. You can also learn about different kinds of printer, monitor, and mouse.

storing information on a computer

The hardware of a computer is the actual bits it is made up of. Besides the hardware, a computer needs software (the programs that tell it what to do).

a computer's brains

A computer's brains

At the heart of any computer is the central processing unit (the CPU). This is the computer's 'brain'. It does all the millions of calculations that a computer can do every second. In a modern computer, the CPU is a microprocessor – a tiny piece of silicon that contains thousands of tiny transistors and other electronic bits.

The CPU is part of something called the motherboard. This connects the CPU up to all the other bits of the computer and controls the information going into and out of the CPU. Without the motherboard there would be information 'traffic jams', and the whole computer would crash.

Memory

Besides doing calculations, a computer has to be able to store information. Anything that needs to be kept for a long time is stored on the hard drive. This is a stack of small metal disks that can store information magnetically. The disks spin thousands of times every second. A magnetic head just above the disk surface reads and writes information to and from the disk.

If information only needs to be stored for a short time, it is stored in the random-access memory (RAM). This is where the computer stores information temporarily, while it is doing a particular job.

The big difference between RAM and the hard drive is that if you turn the computer off, the information stored in the RAM is lost. This is why it is very important to save your work. Saving a file moves information from the RAM to the hard drive.

computer memory

Peripherals

Besides the computing part itself, a computer needs other bits of hardware called peripherals. Peripherals can be input devices (ways to put information into the computer) or output devices (ways to get information out of the computer), or both. The keyboard is the main input device. You use the keyboard to type information or commands into the computer.

peripherals

The other important input device is the mouse. It controls the movement of the cursor on the computer screen. You can also click the mouse to give the computer commands.

A computer's main output device is the monitor (the screen). On screen you can look at anything from movies to schoolwork. Most monitors also have speakers so that you can hear sounds.

There are two kinds of monitor. The old-fashioned kind are called CRT (cathode ray tube) screens. They are big and heavy, and look like old TVs. Newer monitors have flatter, lighter screens called TFT (thin film transfer) or LCD (liquid crystal display) screens.

Other hardware

There are many other peripherals that you can use with your computer. Printers print out copies of files on to paper. A scanner can scan in pictures and other information from a book or magazine and store it on the computer. CDs and DVDs can store information away from the computer itself. You can also link up your computer with a digital camera or a webcam, a microphone, a mobile phone, or a whole range of other devices.

CPU p10 • DVD p17 • hard disk p18
keyboard p18 • memory p19
monitor p19 • mouse p19
printer p21 • scanner p21
software p24 • webcam p47

cable

Cables are the wires that connect different parts of a computer system to each other.

CD (compact disc)

A CD is a device for storing music or other kinds of information. There are several kinds. A CD-ROM is a CD that you can read information from, but you can't write to. A CD-RW is one that you can write to as well as read. CDs are the most popular method of storing or backing up data away from the computer.

external memory p17

a read-write CD (CD-RW)

circuit board

A circuit board is a small piece of plastic with electronic circuits on it. Usually the circuit board will include at least one microchip.

microchip p12

compatible

When pieces of computer equipment are compatible, they can work together.

control devices

Control devices are things such as the mouse and the keyboard, which allow you to communicate with the computer.

mouse p19 • keyboard p18

CRT (cathode ray tube)

A CRT is a kind of monitor screen. CRT screens are big and heavy, like old-fashioned TV sets. Most computers now have flat screens.

device

A device is a separate piece of equipment that can be wired up to a computer. Monitors, printers, scanners, and keyboards are all devices.

disk

Computer disks are used to store information. The hard disk in the computer is one kind of disk. Floppy disks, CDs, and DVDs are other kinds of disk.

floppy disk p17 • hard disk p18

dot matrix printer

A dot matrix printer uses tiny dots to form letters. These dots are produced by tiny pins hitting an ink ribbon. Dot matrix printers cannot produce high quality printing, but they are fast and cheap to run.

DVD (Digital Versatile Disc)

A DVD is similar to a CD, but it can hold much more information. Computer games, films, and music videos often come on DVDs.

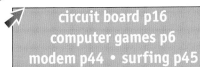
computer games p6 • CD p16

expansion card

An expansion card is an extra circuit board that can be plugged into a slot inside the computer. This makes it possible to add extra facilities such as a graphics card to make computer games more fun, or a better modem to make surfing faster.

circuit board p16
computer games p6
modem p44 • surfing p45

expansion slot

An expansion slot is a space inside a computer where extra memory, or an expansion card, can be fitted.

external memory

External memory is any method of storing information outside the computer. Floppy disks used to be the main way to do this. Nowadays there are lots of different kinds of external memory. The one people use most is CDs. They hold much more information than a floppy disk. DVDs are another kind of external memory.

You can also use a tape drive, a zip drive, a pen drive, or a separate hard disk.

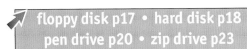
floppy disk p17 • hard disk p18
pen drive p20 • zip drive p23

floor turtle

A floor turtle is a small turtle-like robot that can be controlled using a computer. It is used to teach basic programming skills to young children.

program p30

floppy disk

A floppy disk is one kind of external memory (a way of storing information away from the computer). The original floppy disks were round and floppy. Today the disk is protected in a plastic case. Floppy disks can only hold small amounts of information compared with CDs or DVDs. It also takes much longer to move files to and from a floppy disk.

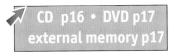
CD p16 • DVD p17
external memory p17

hard copy

A hard copy is a printed version of information stored on your computer.

hard disk

The hard disk on a computer is where all the information is stored. The disk is about 9 centimetres across and spins at very high speed. The information is stored in a magnetic coating on the surface of the disk. You can also buy hard disk drives separately, to use as external storage.

external memory p 17

heat sink

A heat sink is a part of the computer that stops the CPU from getting too hot by conducting heat away from it.

CPU p10

inkjet printer

An inkjet printer is the most common type of printer. It prints pictures and photographs by spraying the surface of the paper with millions of microscopic dots of coloured ink.

printer p21

jewel case

A jewel case is a transparent plastic case for storing a CD.

CD p16

joystick

A joystick is a type of game controller. It is a handle that you can move to control or steer objects on the screen.

keyboard

The keyboard is the main way of putting information into a computer. It looks very similar to an old-fashioned typewriter keyboard. It is called a QWERTY keyboard because the first six letter keys spell 'QWERTY'. A keyboard can be used to write on the computer. It can also be used to give the computer commands, using keyboard shortcuts and function keys.

keyboard

laptop

A laptop is a portable computer not much bigger than a book. It is powered by batteries so you can use it any-where. There is also a mains lead for charging up the batteries and for using the laptop at home.

laser printer

A laser printer is an alternative to an inkjet printer. It is faster than an inkjet, but it costs more. Laser printers are usually found in offices rather than in the home.

printer p21

LCD (liquid crystal display)

An LCD screen is the type used in laptops and in flat monitors. LCDs were first used for things like the displays on calculators and digital watches.

> laptop p18 • monitor p19

Macintosh

A Macintosh, or Apple Mac, is one of the two main types of computer. The other is the PC (a computer that runs using the Microsoft Windows operating system). Macintosh computers are made by the computer company Apple. Macs are popular with designers and people recording music or making videos on computers.

> operating system p30
> PC p20 • Windows p31

magnetic disk

Magnetic disks are used in computers to store data (information). The hard drive is a magnetic disk.

> hard disk p17

memory

A computer's memory is the place where it stores information for a short time. This kind of temporary memory is also called RAM (random-access memory). When you turn the computer off, you lose any information stored in the memory, unless you have saved it to the hard disk.

> hard disk p18

microprocessor

A microprocessor is another name for the central processing unit (CPU) of a computer.

> CPU p10

monitor

A computer monitor looks similar to a television screen. It is the main way in which your computer communicates with the outside world. Some computers, such as laptops, have a screen built into them. Other computers have a separate monitor. There are two kinds of monitor. Older computers have large, heavy CRT screens. Newer computers have LCD screens that are thinner and lighter.

> CRT p16 • LCD p19 • laptop p18

mouse

A mouse is one of a computer's two main input devices. The other is the keyboard. The mouse controls the cursor (pointer) on the computer screen. A mouse can have two or sometimes three buttons, all of which do different things. Some mice also have a wheel, which you can use to scroll up and down the screen.

> device p16 • cursor p52

mouse

19

notebook

A notebook is a small portable computer, about the size of a notebook.

palmtop

A palmtop is a tiny computer which – you've guessed it – can be held in the palm of your hand.

PC (personal computer)

A PC is the kind of computer you have on your desk, rather than a portable one such as a laptop or a notebook. It is the kind of computer that most people own or use at work. Computers that use Microsoft Windows as an operating system are also called PCs.

laptop 18 • Macintosh p19
notebook p20
operating system p30

pen drive

A pen drive is a way of carrying documents and files from one computer to another. A pen drive is no bigger than a very fat pen, but some kinds can store up to a gigabyte of information. Pen drives are also known as memory sticks, data keys, flash memory, and USB drives.

gigabyte p11 • USB p59

peripheral

A peripheral is anything that is not part of the actual computer itself. Monitors, printers, scanners, keyboards, and mice are all peripherals.

keyboard p18 • monitor p19
mouse p19 • printer p21
scanner p21

peripherals

plug and play

A plug-and-play device is one that you can just plug into your computer, and it works automatically.

pen drive

printer

A printer is a machine for turning information from a computer into 'hard copy' (words or pictures on paper). The most common kinds of printer today are inkjet and laser printers. Most people use inkjet printers at home because they are cheaper and work well for most purposes. Businesses and people who use printers a lot choose laser printers, because they are better quality, work faster and last longer.

laser printer p18
inkjet printer p18

processor

A processor is another name for a microprocessor.

microprocessor p19

RAM (ramdom access memory)

RAM is a computer's short-term memory.

memory p19

removable disk

A removable disk such as a CD can be stored away from the computer. This is different from a hard drive, which is usually part of the computer.

ROM (read only memory)

ROM is information that is stored permanently on a computer's processor and is used when you 'boot up' (start) the computer. ROM cannot be altered: it is 'read-only'. Unlike RAM, the information is not lost when the computer closes down.

RAM p21

scanner

A scanner is a machine that allows you to put pictures on to a computer. You put the picture you want to save on the scanner, and it scans the image with a special light. The scanner saves the information in a picture file, which your computer can read and understand.

file p54

sensor

A sensor is a device that can pick up and measure changes in the environment (for example, changes in temperature or light levels). The equipment then saves the measurements electronically, in a way that can be read by a computer.

sensor

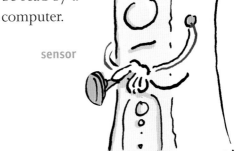

server

A server is a computer that holds information that can be accessed by a number of computers on a network.

access p61 • network p44

sound card

A sound card is just what it says, a circuit board that allows you to play sound on your computer. A sound card is vital if you play music or games on your computer. Most computers come with a sound card installed.

circuit board p16 • install p29

sound card

storage

Storage is the name for any device that you can use to store information on a computer. There are three types of storage. Fixed storage, such as the hard drive, is part of the computer itself. Removable storage is something like a CD, a DVD, or a pen drive. These can all be taken out of the computer. Finally,

there is temporary storage, such as RAM memory. In this kind of storage the information is lost when you switch the computer off.

CD p16 • DVD p17
hard disk p18 • pen drive p20
RAM p21

storage

terminal

A terminal is a piece of equipment such as a keyboard and screen that lets you work on a computer somewhere else. Several terminals can be connected to the same computer.

TFT (thin film transfer)

This is another name for a flat, liquid crystal (LCD) computer screen.

LCD p19

touch screen

A touch screen computer is one where you give commands by touching areas of the screen instead of using a mouse. Touch screens are often seen at train stations, where they are used for ordering tickets. They are also used for interactive displays in museums. At one time people thought that touch screens might take over from the mouse. But sitting all day with an arm outstretched to touch the screen becomes very uncomfortable. Most people still prefer to use a mouse.

 mouse p19

tracker ball

A tracker ball is a kind of upside-down computer mouse. On a mechanical mouse, a moving ball on the bottom controls the movement of the pointer on the computer screen. On a tracker ball, the ball is placed on the top, where it is controlled by the movement of a person's hand. This saves space, as there is no need to move the whole device around.

 mouse p19

workstation

A workstation is a single computer that is connected to a network.

 network p44

zip drive

A zip drive is a type of external storage. You put a zip disk into the drive, and use this to store information, as with a CD or DVD. However, unlike a CD or DVD, you can use a zip disk again and again.

A computer without software is like a torch without batteries, or a carriage without a horse. It's not really much good for anything! Software is all the programs that a computer needs to work properly. The software feature explains about the different types of software, and about how computer programmers put together new software. The other features tell you more about different kinds of software, from Acrobat to Word. There is also information about words that programmers use, such as installing and uninstalling, protocol and workaround.

applications software for making music, writing, and painting

Acrobat

Acrobat is a computer program that 'freezes' all the different parts of your document in place. This means your project or poster will look exactly the same on another computer. You can convert documents made in many different programs into Acrobat programs.

PDF p30 • program p30

address harvester

An address harvester is a program which collects or 'harvests' email addresses from the Internet. People use them in various ways. Most often they are used to send spam – annoying or dodgy emails that clog up your inbox.

email p39
Internet p33 • spam p86

address harvester

algorithm

An algorithm is an exact set of instructions that carries out a particular task on a computer.

applet

An applet is a small program that can run on a web page. Applets are often used for short animations (moving pictures).

web page p47 • program p30

application

An application is the type of computer program that helps you to do something, rather than one that helps to run the computer. Wordpad is an application that helps you to write a letter, while Paint is a drawing application.

back door

A back door is a way around the security of a program that is deliberately left by its designers. This is so that technicians who might need to tweak the program can get into it without having to use the standard passwords.

security p82

back door

Software is the name for the sets of instructions or programs that a computer needs to carry out even the smallest task. Unlike computer hardware, which you can see and shout at, software is invisible.

Binary numbers

Computers cannot be programmed simply by typing instructions, or even with ordinary numbers. For a computer to understand something, it has to be written using binary numbers. Instead of using the numbers 1 to 10, binary numbers use only the numbers 1 and 0 to store information. A computer stores information using millions of electronic switches. It can store binary numbers easily because 1 equals 'switch on' and 0 equals 'switch off'.

Although computers have no trouble working with binary numbers, it is very difficult to write out every instruction in binary code. Instead, people have created special programming languages, such as BASIC and HTML. These make it much easier to write instructions for a computer.

Types of software

All computers come with some basic programs already built into them. These programs are called system software, or the operating system. These programs do things such as creating the desktop, which makes it possible to communicate with the computer through the keyboard and mouse. Most home PCs use the Microsoft Windows operating system, while Macintosh computers use the Apple operating system.

binary numbers

The operating system makes it possible to load application software. The application software is all the programs that allow you to do things on the computer. Word processing and graphics programs, computer games, music software, internet browsers, databases and spreadsheet programs are all types of application software.

spreadsheet

Easter egg

As a bit of relief from all their hard work, software writers sometimes hide small programs called 'Easter eggs' within the main program. The Easter egg is often a short animation that can only be activated by pressing a secret combination of keys.

Writing software

Most people can learn to write simple programs for a computer. At school you may have learned to program the movements of a turtle on the computer screen. But writing applications programs for modern computers is extremely complex. Many different people work on them. Early versions of a new program are tested out by many different users to find any 'bugs' or faults. Even then there are often problems with a brand new piece of software.

database

careware

Careware is software that you can download freely from the Internet on the condition that you make a donation to charity.

Internet p33

configure

When you configure your computer you set it up so that it suits your particular way of working. For instance, you might choose a new colour scheme for your computer or you might choose a different background for your desktop.

background p50 • desktop p53

configure

DOS (disk operating system)

An operating system is the program that looks after the basic running of a computer. DOS is the operating system used in most PCs.

operating system p30

driver

A driver is a small program that your computer needs to communicate with other pieces of equipment such as printers or scanners. Each piece of equipment works in its own particular way, so it needs its own driver. The driver usually comes on a CD with the equipment.

CD p16 • program p30

Easter egg

An Easter egg is a little animation or game that the designers of software sometimes hide in a program for fun. To get at the Easter egg you have to have a special password.

password p85 • program p30

Easter egg

encode

To encode, or encrypt, something means to put it into a code that cannot be read by other people. Personal information held on the Internet, such as people's bank details, is encoded to stop other people from reading it.

Internet p33

Excel

Excel is a well-known spreadsheet program. It can be used for things like creating lists and tables. It is mainly used for working with financial data.

> data p80 • spreadsheet p81

Excel

executable file

An executable (.exe) file is one that runs itself when you click on it. Installation programs are usually .exe files. Viruses that are sent over the Internet are often .exe files.

> file p54 • install p29

Flash

Flash is a type of animation program used on the web. Many Internet computer games are programmed in Flash.

> program p30 • Internet p33

freeware

Freeware is software that is given away completely free on the Internet.

icebreaker

An icebreaker is a type of program designed to crack the security of another program.

> security p82

import

To import data is to open files or information created in one program in a different program.

> data p80 • program p30

install

When a program is installed on to a computer it is put into its memory. Once a program has been installed, you can use it.

> memory p19 • program p30

Java

Java is a programming language widely used on the Internet.

Software

Javascript

Javascript is a programming language that allows websites to be more interactive.

operating system (OS)

The operating system is a group of programs that do the basic running of a computer. The operating system does things like setting up the desktop, which allows you to communicate with the computer using the keyboard and the mouse. Microsoft Windows is the operating system that runs most PCs.

desktop p53 • PC p20
Windows p31

patch

A patch is a small piece of software added to a program to cure a problem.

PDF (portable document format)

PDF files are ones made with a program called Acrobat. You can convert documents made in many different programs into PDF files.

Acrobat p25

pendown

Pendown is a command you can use to program a floor turtle. It causes the turtle to draw a line as it moves.

floor turtle p17

Powerpoint

Microsoft Powerpoint is a well-known presentation programme. It is used to create presentations with images, charts, video, and sound.

program

A program is another word for software. It is a group of instructions that tell a computer how to carry out a particular job.

protocol

A protocol is a set of rules that allows computers to communicate and exchange information with each other. For instance, when computers send emails they use the Post Office Protocol (POP), and when they receive emails they use the Simple Mail Transport Protocol (SMTP).

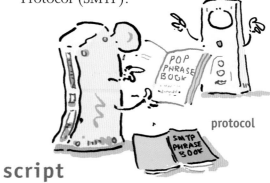
protocol

script

A script is a piece of computer code that does a small task. For instance, in a database program you could make a script to call up all the records beginning with the letter 'A' when you click a button on the screen.

database p80

software

shareware

Shareware is computer software that is free to try, but after a trial period you must pay to use it.

uninstall

To uninstall a program means to remove it completely from your computer. Most applications come with a special uninstall program to do this.

 install p29

UNIX

UNIX is one type of computer operating system. It is often used for servers on the internet.

operating system p30
server p22

upload

To upload a file or a program means to copy it from your computer to a website.

website p47

upload

vapourware

Vapourware is software that has been announced by a manufacturer but not yet released.

vapourware

Windows®

Windows (with a capital W) is the name of the Microsoft operating system that is used on most PCs.

 operating system p30 • PC p20

winkey

A winkey is an emoticon that looks like a winking face if you look at it sideways on: **;)**

 emoticon p101

WinZip

WinZip is a program that compresses files so that they take up less space on the computer.

 compress p51

wizard

A wizard is a program that guides you through a task, step by step. For instance, you might use a wizard in a spreadsheet program to help you create a graph or chart.

Word

Microsoft Word is the name of the most common word-processing program.

 **word processing p65**

workaround

A workaround is a method of getting round a problem in a program without having to rewrite large bits of it.

program p30

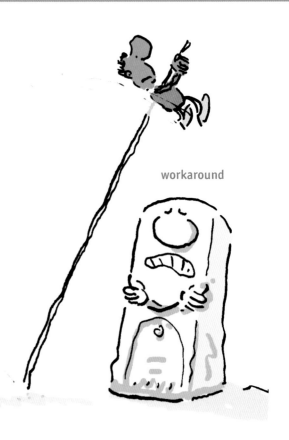

workaround

ICT and the Internet

We don't just use computers at home. You find them everywhere, in shops, offices, and factories, in airliners and trains, even in traffic lights. The article on ICT is about the many different ways we use computers.

People have only been able to use the Internet since the 1980s, but in a short time it has become one of the most important parts of computing. The Internet feature tells you something about the history of the Internet and the many different things that people use it for. There is also an article on emails, which explains what happens when you send an email to a friend. The other entries tell you about attachments and downloads, broadband and dial-up, newsgroups and chat rooms.

surfing the Internet

ICT

ICT stands for Information and Communication Technology. It is about all the different ways that people use computers, and what they use them for.

ICT at home or school

You probably use a computer at home or at school. You might write a story on it, or draw a picture. A story is easier to change and correct if you write it using ICT. With a picture, you can copy the bits you like and use them again, or change the colours really easily.

You can also store data (information) on a computer. You might have an address book on your computer, with the contact information for all your friends. With ICT, you can organise the data in different ways. You might want to list your friends in order of their first names. Or you might want to list them in your own order, perhaps with your best friends first. Changing data about is easy with ICT.

You might also use computers for communication. Using the Internet, it's as easy to email a penpal in Greenland as it is to contact a friend down the road. You can also use the Internet to help with your school work.
One other thing you probably do with ICT is have fun. You can play computer games, write and draw, play music, or watch a video.

ICT all around you

Everywhere you go you will see ICT systems being used in different ways. Some ICT systems are used to manage data (information). In shops there are barcodes on all the products. An ICT system uses these barcodes to keep track of everything. The shop manager can see which things are selling well and need re-ordering. Sometimes the ICT system can also do the ordering. Other ICT systems control machines. Factories making cars, aircraft, electronics, and many other things rely on computers to control the machines. In a car factory, computers control robot arms that do things like cut out car parts and weld them together.

emailing a penpal

ICT systems are also used for communications. They transport data from one place to another. Emails and telephone systems, TV, radio, and the Internet are all communications systems that rely on computers.

ICT criminals

computer hacker

Computers are very useful for doing all kinds of things. But some people have found ways to use ICT to steal and cause trouble. Hackers crack the codes that protect people's computer information. They cause trouble by sending out viruses, or by stealing important information. And some criminals have worked out ways to steal money from banks using computers.

Improved computers

Today's computer systems are far better than they were 40 years ago. A modern DVD can hold the same amount of information as 1400 computer disks from the 1960s. Because computers are so much better, we use them more and more in our daily lives. Maybe tomorrow we won't need PCs at all. We will be able to use a pocket computer that can do everything a PC can do, plus much more.

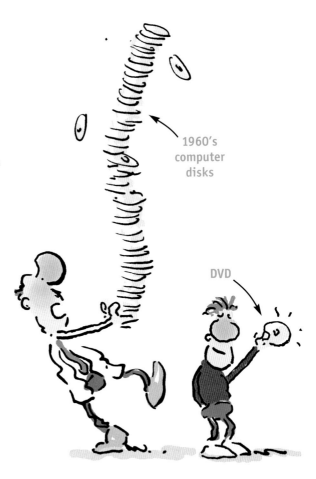

1960's computer disks

DVD

address

The address of a website is the string of letters or numbers that take you to that website. The address is divided into several parts, separated by slashes and dots. For instance, in the web address, www.thispage.com, the first part, www., stands for world wide web. This is in most web addresses. The second part ('thispage') is the 'domain' name – the actual name of this particular website. The last part describes the type of domain it is. The 'com' in this example is short for 'company'. The ending 'org' means 'organisation', while 'uk' is the ending for a UK website.

 website p47 • world wide web p48

address

address book

The address book is the part of an email program where you can keep the email addresses, phone numbers, and other contact details of your friends.

 **email p39**

ADSL (Asymetric Digital Subscriber Line)

ADSL is a way of sending digital data from one place to another along a telephone line. With ADSL, the telephone and the Internet can work at the same time on the same phone line. Broadband internet connections use ADSL.

broadband p37 • data p80 digital p10 • Internet p33

attachment

An attachment is a file that you attach to an email. This can be a picture, a program, or some writing. Computer viruses are often spread in attachments, so it is best not to open attachments in emails from people you don't know.

email p39 • program p30 virus p86

backbone

The backbone is an important part of the internet. It is the 'main highway' for information travelling through the Internet.

bandwidth

Bandwidth is the amount of information your Internet connection can handle. The wider the bandwidth, the faster you can surf the web.

 Internet p33 • surf p45 world wide web p48

blog/blogger

A blog is a personal diary or journal published on the Internet. A blogger is someone who writes a blog.

bottom feeder

Bottom feeder is the name given to the sort of person who spends their time surfing the internet looking for free stuff, such as free programs, fonts, or music.

program p30 • font p62

bps (bits per second)

This is the standard way of measuring how quickly data (information) can be sent between computers over the Internet. The higher the bps the faster you can download and upload. This becomes important if you want to exchange picture or music files. These files are usually quite big.

**bit p3 • data p80
download p38 • upload p31**

broadband

Broadband is a way of connecting to the Internet using an ordinary phone line. A broadband connection works much faster than dial-up networking. Broadband also lets you use the phone and the Internet at the same time.

dial-up networking p38

broken link

A broken link is a link to a web page or site that no longer works.

web page p47 • website p47

browser

A browser is a program you can use to look at websites and to find your way around the Internet. The best known browser is called Internet Explorer.

program p30

bulletin board

A bulletin board is a place on the Internet that displays messages or notices that can be read by people.

CAM (computer-aided manufacturing)

CAM means making things with the help of computers. Computers control how all kinds of things are made. For instance, they are used to control robots that weld the different parts of a car together.

chat rooms

Chat rooms are areas on the Internet where people with similar interests can 'chat', or exchange ideas. The best are those run by well-known names such as Microsoft or AOL where you have your own personal password and username.

password p85 • username p46

cobweb site

A cobweb site is an old website that is so out of date it has grown whiskers.

cobweb site

cookies

Cookies are little pieces of information that a website leaves on your computer. This means that if you return to the website it will already know some of your likes and dislikes. For instance, a music site might know that you prefer solo singers to bands.

website p47

dead link

A dead link is a link to a web page that leads nowhere, usually because the website no longer exists.

website p47

dial-up networking

Dial-up networking is a way of connecting to the Internet using a modem and an ordinary telephone line. Dial-up connection to the Internet

is slow. Many people now have a broadband connection.

broadband p37 • Internet p33
modem p44

domain name

The domain name is another name for the address of a website.

address p36

www.cosynook.co.uk

domain name

download

To download is to copy information from an outside source (usually the Internet) to your computer. People download things like music, ringtones, and programs. You need to be sure that the place you are downloading from is safe, or you may end up with a virus on your computer.

program p30 • virus p86

e-commerce

E-commerce is the word used to describe buying and selling on the Internet. eBay is a popular website for buying and selling online.

The first real email was only sent in 1971, but now 22 million emails are sent every day. The first emails were only text. Today documents, pictures, music and even short videos can be sent as attachments to an email. Emails have become the world's most popular form of communication.

sending an email

Sending an email

When you send an email, it travels from your computer to the computer of the friend you are emailing. To do this it uses the Internet. First the email goes from your computer to an email server. The server is like a sorting office for emails. It is connected to the Internet. Most people with home computers send emails through their Internet service provider (ISP). Big companies and other places with lots of computers often have their own email server that connects to the Internet.

From here, the email travels through the Internet to the server of your friend. The server stores the mail until your friend decides to look at their emails. Then the email is downloaded on to their computer.

An email address is divided into two parts. The first part is the name of the person whose email it is. The part that comes after the @ sign is the address of their email server.

Spam and viruses

One of the biggest problems with email is spam, or unwanted email. Every year 4 billion spam messages are sent. This is half of all the emails sent in a year. Spam is usually just a nuisance, but sometimes it can be very unpleasant. Most spam is sent by just a few people, but it is hard to catch them. They could be based anywhere on Earth.

Emails are also the most common way of infecting computers with viruses. Viruses are tiny programs designed to cause problems on your computer. They are usually sent attached to an innocent-seeming email message. The safest way to avoid viruses is to install anti-virus software on your computer. It is also best not to open an email message or attachment from someone that you don't know.

antivirus software p83
attachment p36 • install p29
program p30 • server p22
spam p86 • virus p86

39

egosurf

To egosurf is to search the Internet hoping to find your name mentioned or to find links to your website.

website p47

egosurf

e-zine

An e-zine is a magazine that you can read on the Internet.

forum

A forum is another word for a newsgroup or a chat room.

newsgroup p44 • chat room p37

frame

A frame divides a web page into different areas, each of which acts like a separate web page.

web page p47

fibre optics

Fibre optics, or optical fibres, are 'wires' made from lots of very thin strands of glass. Fibre optic cables can be used to send information from place to place, in a similar way to ordinary telephone wires. However, they are much faster than normal wires, and can carry more information. An ordinary wire sends information as changing patterns of electricity. Optical fibres send the information as patterns of light.

FTP (file transfer protocol)

This is a way to transfer files from one computer to another, usually via the Internet.

file p54

gateway

A gateway is a device that connects one or more computers on a network to the internet, or to some other network.

ghost site

A ghost site is a deserted website that has been abandoned but hasn't been removed from the Internet.

website p47

ghost site

Google

Google is the name of a well-known search engine. People use Google to make over 170 000 000 searches a day.

search engine p45

Googlewacking

Googlewacking is a game played using the Google search engine. The idea is to use just two words for a Google search and get back exactly one result. There are websites dedicated to this new sport.

search engine p45 • website p47

gopher

A gopher is a simple program used for finding information on the internet. Gophers were used to find information on the internet before search engines became common.

handshake

A handshake is the series of signals a modem makes when you have a dial-up connection to the internet. It sounds a bit like fingernails scratching and scraping down a blackboard.

dial-up networking p38
modem p44

hit

A hit is another term for a visit to a website.

home page

The home page is the first page you see when you go to a website. Your home page is the one that comes up when you first connect to the Internet.

website p47

home page

host

A host computer stores information that a group of other computers have access to.

access p61

hotlink

A hotlink is a link between two different programs. Changing information in one program will affect the other.

program p30

hot spot

A hot spot is a public area such as an airport where computers with wireless networking can get on to the Internet and send emails.

wireless network p47

html (hypertext markup language)

This is the language that is used to write most web pages. If you go to an html web page and from the View menu choose 'Source', you can see the html code for that web page.

http (hypertext transfer protocol)

This is the name for the code or language that computers use to send information over the Internet. Most Internet addresses begin 'http://'.

 address p36

hyperlink

A hyperlink allows you to jump from place to place in a website or a document simply by clicking on a highlighted word or phrase. Thumbnail pictures sometimes have hyperlinks too, that take you to a bigger version of the picture.

 document p62 • website p47

hypertext

Hypertext is a document or piece of text containing hyperlinks.

information superhighway

The information superhighway is another name for the Internet.

Internet address

Internet address is another name for an address.

 address p36

Internet worm

An Internet worm is a harmful program sent over the Internet. It spreads by producing copies of itself.

intranet

An intranet is a miniature version of the Internet that is used to share information. Businesses, universities, and other organisations often have their own intranet.

IP address

The IP address is the individual address of a computer connected to the Internet.

 address p36

ISP (Internet service provider)

An ISP is a company that provides you with a connection to the Internet. ISPs usually provide lots of extras such as news and chat rooms.

 chat room p37

LAN (local area network)

LAN is the name for a small network of computers.

link

A link is the same as a hyperlink.

link rot

Link rot is when links from one web page to another gradually stop working as the pages they link to gradually change or disappear.

mail exploder

A mail exploder is a piece of software that sends the same email to many different email addresses.

mail storm

A mail storm is a flood of incoming emails that overload a computer and stop it working properly.

email p39

mailbox

A mailbox is a file that only receives the email of one particular person. This is handy when several people use the same computer.

microwaves

Microwaves are invisible rays similar to radio waves. Microwaves are used by mobile phones to send information, because they can travel long distances without any loss of quality.

mirror site

A mirror site is an exact copy of an existing website. Websites that are visited a lot often have a mirror site. When the original site is too busy, people can visit the mirror site instead. Websites where you can download things often have mirror sites in several different parts of the world. This is because downloads are quicker from a nearby website.

download p38 • website p47

mail storm

modem

A modem is a circuit board that connects your computer to the Internet. It communicates with other computers in the special language developed for the Internet, called http.

 circuit board p16 • http p42

MSN

MSN Messenger is a way to chat online using text, voice, or even video conversation in real time.

navigating

To navigate means to find your way around. You might navigate around a computer or the Internet.

network

A network is a group of computers that are connected to each other.

network card

A network card is a circuit board that connects a computer to a network.

 circuit board p16

newsgroup

A newsgroup is a group of people who exchange ideas and views over the Internet, using a bulletin board. This is an area on the Internet where members of the newsgroup can read messages or post (write) their own.

offline

When you are offline, you are not connected to the Internet.

online

When you are online, you are connected to the Internet.

ping

A ping is a signal sent over the Internet by a computer to check that another computer is communicating correctly.

pipe

A pipe is a connection to the Internet.

portal

A portal is a website that acts as a 'gateway' to other services on the Internet. Most portals include things like a search engine, email, newsgroups, chat rooms, and online shopping. Your Internet home page is probably a portal containing all kinds of useful information.

chat room p37 • email p39
newsgroup p44
search engine p45 • website p47

newsgroup

router

A router is a piece of equipment that works out the best way to send information through a computer network.

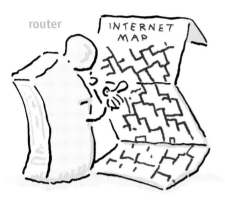

router

surf

To surf means to explore the Internet for interesting websites.

surfing

search engine

A search engine is a special program that makes gathering information from the Internet far easier. You type the word or phrase that you want to search for in the search engine window, then click on the search button. The search engine looks on the Internet and finds a list of websites that have the search words in them.

program p30

telecommunications

Telecommunications is a word for any kind of long-distance communication using radio waves or microwaves. Mobile phones, telephones, television, radio, and the Internet all use telecommunications to send information from one place to another.

microwaves p43

spider

A spider is a program that is part of a search engine. It searches the Internet for new websites.

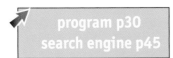

program p30
search engine p45

spider

teleconferencing

Teleconferencing is a way to hold meetings between people who are not all in the same place. Each person or group of people has a webcam, a microphone, and a computer hooked up to the Internet. People on opposite sides of the world can meet and talk this way.

webcam p47

teleconferencing

URL (uniform resource locator)

An URL is another word for an Internet address.

usenet

The usenet is a worldwide network of computer systems. All the newsgroups on the Internet are maintained by the usenet.

newsgroup p44

username

Your username is a name that is used to identify you when you go on the Internet or another computer network. Usually you need a password as well as a username to be able to use the network.

network p44 • password p85

WAP (wireless application protocol)

WAP is the method that some mobile phones use to connect to the Internet.

webmaster

A webmaster is someone who looks after the running of a website. They are also called web administrators. A webmaster may design and build the website in the first place. They make sure that the web pages are kept up to date, and deal with any problems if something on the website goes wrong.

web page p47 • website p47

webmaster

website

A website is a collection of web pages about a single topic, or produced by a person or an organisation. There are billions of websites on the Internet. They are about everything from aardvarks to zucchini.

 web page p47

web page

A web page is a single page on the world wide web.

 world wide web p48

webcam

A webcam is a small video camera that you can use with your computer.

web space

Web space is the amount of space a website takes up on the Internet. If you have an Internet service provider (ISP), they will usually give you a certain amount of free web space so that you can put up your own website.

website p47

WiFi

WiFi is another name for a wireless network.

wireless network

wireless network

A wireless network is a network of computers that do not need wires to communicate with each other. Each computer has a wireless card, which can send out information using radio signals rather than wires. All the computers send their signals to a central router, which sends the information on to the right place. The router is usually connected to the Internet.

router p45

web space

world wide web

The world wide web (or 'the web') is the huge network of billions of web pages on the Internet. The web was begun in 1989, when a man called Tim Berners-Lee developed a special language called http. This is a way for computers to connect together and understand each other. Most web documents are written in html. This is a coding language that all computers on the web can understand. Users can look at pages on the web using a web browser program such as Internet Explorer or Netscape.

 browser p37 • html p42 http p42 • web page p47

XML (extensible markup language)

XML is a computer language for creating Web documents.

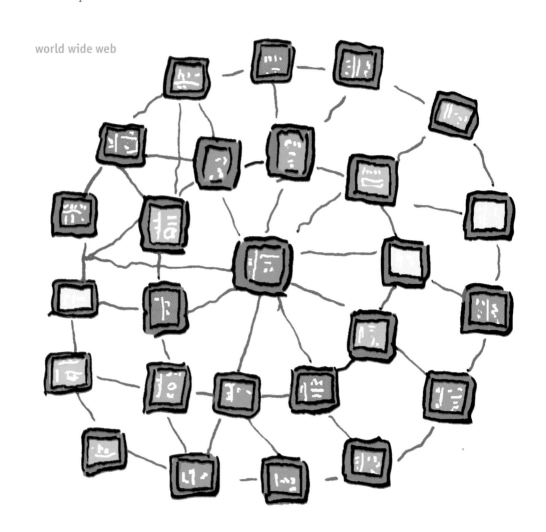

world wide web

ICT and the Internet

Using a computer

This section is all about the bits of your computer that are not concerned with specific programs, such as the desktop, windows, menu, toolbars, folders, and files. There are also entries on computer housekeeping, such as backing up files and defragmenting your hard drive. You can find out about things that go wrong, such as crashing, hanging, and fatal errors. Do you know the difference between a boot and a warm boot? Can you tell a serial port from a parallel port? Find out all about it in this section.

getting information
out of a computer port

active window

The active window is the window on a computer screen that you are working on. If more than one window is open, the active window is on top.

> ↗ **window p59**

alias

An alias is a nickname that you can remember easily. It is used in place of an email address. On Macintosh computers, an alias is a shortcut to a particular file or folder.

> ↗ **address p36 • file p54**
> **folder p54 • shortcut p58**

archive

To archive files is to put files you don't use very much into an archive folder, or on to a CD or floppy disk. This is rather like clearing your old clothes into the attic and making room for more. It gives you more space on the computer and makes it run better.

> ↗ **CD p16 • floppy disk p17**

background

Many computer programs can work in the background. Your printer can usually work in the background too. This means that the computer can do a job in one program, or print something out, while you are doing something else in another program.

> ↗ **program p30 • printer p21**

backing up

Backing up is what sensible people do before they clean their teeth at night. It means saving a copy of the work on your computer to a CD or other kind of external memory. Then, if your computer goes up in a puff of smoke while you're asleep, your life's work doesn't go with it.

> ↗ **external memory p17**
> **memory p19**

backspace

You'll find the backspace key on the top right of your keyboard, marked 'Backspace' or 'Bk Sp'. The backspace key moves the cursor arrow back one space at a time, deleting any letters that happen to be in its way.

> ↗ **cursor p52 • keyboard p18**

batch file

A batch file is a file containing a group, or 'batch', of commands that are carried out together. Batch files can be used to install a set of programs on to a computer's hard disk.

> ↗ **command p67 • hard disk p18**
> **install p29 • program p30**

bookmark

Bookmarks are shortcuts to your favourite web pages. If you bookmark a web page, the computer remembers the web address and takes you straight there when you click on the bookmark. Some word processing programs also use bookmarks so that you can mark important places in a long file.

 favourites p54 • web page p47

boot

To boot up your computer is to start it up.

boot up your computer

buttons

Buttons are one way of showing files on your desktop or in a window. When you click on a button, it takes you to a particular file or opens a program.

 **window p59**

cache

The cache is a part of a computer's temporary memory, or RAM, used to store frequently accessed information. This helps a program perform more efficiently.

 **RAM p21**

clipboard

The clipboard is a part of the RAM or temporary memory. When you copy a piece of information, it is stored on the clipboard until you paste it somewhere else.

 **copy and paste p62**

compress

If you compress a file, you make it smaller. A compressed file takes up less space on the computer. It is also much quicker to send over the internet. Compression is particularly good when you want to email big files such as pictures, music, or movies.

compressing files  **email p39**

context-sensitive menu

This is the list you see when you right-click your mouse. The list tells you things that you can do on that particular part of the screen. For instance, if your cursor is over a word, the list might give you the option to change that word to a different font.

 font p62 mouse p19

control panel

The control panel is a set of programs that come with a computer that let you change settings such as the date and time, the way the desktop looks, the speed that the mouse works at, and so on.

 desktop p53 • mouse p19 program p30

crash

A crash is what every computer owner dreads. The computer stops working right in the middle of something important and no amount of pleading will get it to work. The only cure is to turn the computer off and start all over again. You will probably lose any work you haven't saved.

cursor

The cursor is the small arrow or flashing vertical line that shows where the mouse is on your computer screen.

 mouse p19

default

Default settings are the basic factory settings of a new computer or program. For instance, a word processing program will have a default font that it uses unless you change it. You can change these default settings to suit your own taste and way of working.

 **font p62 • program p30 word processing p65**

crash and burn

defragment

To defragment a computer is a bit like spring-cleaning it. When a computer stores information it scatters it in little chunks all across the hard disk and it becomes fragmented. When the computer goes to find a picture of a donkey, the nose might be in one place and the tail in another. Having to look for all the bits slows the computer down. Defragmenting brings the bits of jumbled information back together, so that the computer works more efficiently.

hard disk p18

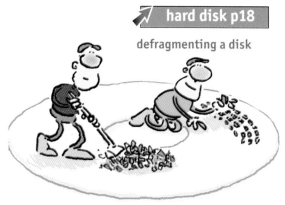

defragmenting a disk

desktop

The desktop is the screen that you first see when you start your computer.

drag and drop

To drag and drop is one way of moving files or folders on your computer. You can move words within a document this way, too. First, you put the mouse cursor over whatever you want to move, then hold down the left mouse button. Now, keep pressing the mouse button as you drag the file or folder to where you want it. Finally, let go of the mouse button to 'drop' the object in its new place.

document p62 • file p54
folder p54

drive

A drive is a place on a computer where you can store information. The computer gives each of these drives a letter. Most computers have a hard disk. This is usually the C drive. There is usually also a slot or tray where you can put in CDs or DVDs, and this is another drive. Some computers have more than one CD drive, or they may have a slot for a floppy disk. And you can attach all kinds of other storage devices to the computer, each of which becomes a separate drive.

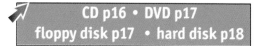

CD p16 • DVD p17
floppy disk p17 • hard disk p18

error

An error is a mistake in a program. It often results in the program closing down.

export

To export data is to move it from one program to another.

data p80

extension

An extension is the group of letters at the end of a file name that lets the computer know what sort of file it is. For instance, a file with the extension '.doc' is a Microsoft Word document.

file p54

fatal error

A fatal error is one that makes a program shut down suddenly. The result is that you often lose whatever you are working on.

error p53

fatal error

favourites

Favourites is another word for bookmarks.

bookmark p51

file

A file is a collection of information stored on your computer. It could contain words, graphics (pictures), music, video, or it could be a database.

database p80

file extension

A file extension is the group of letters after a file's name. The extension tells the computer what kind of file it is. For example, a file with '.doc' at the end is a word processing file made in Microsoft Word. A file with a '.jpg' extension is a picture file.

It is important that file extensions don't get deleted. If they do, the computer might not be able to recognise the file any more.

word processing p65

firewire

Firewire is a way of transferring data rapidly between the computer itself and its peripherals (the bits connected to it, such as the printer or a scanner).

data p80 • peripheral p20

folder

A folder is a collection of files, usually grouped together under a common subject. Organising your files into folders makes life much easier as your computer begins to fill up.

file p54

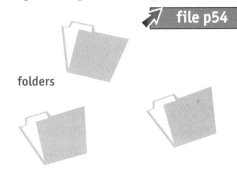

folders

fragmentation

Fragmentation is the way that related pieces of information become separated and scattered across a computer's hard disk. This happens slowly as more information is added to the disk. Eventually, this fragmentation slows the computer down. When this happens, you have to 'defragment' (tidy up) the disk.

 **defragment p53**

hang

When a computer hangs, it suddenly stops what it is doing and waits. Sometimes it is waiting for more information. Sometimes it carries on waiting for ever – in which case it is time to turn off and start again.

hang

import

To import data is to open files or information created in one program in a different program.

inactive window

The inactive window is any window other than the one you are using. Inactive windows appear behind the active window.

interface

An interface is a place where you and the computer communicate.
* Your keyboard is an interface where you can communicate by typing.
* Your mouse is another interface. You move the mouse and click it to communicate with the computer.
* Your monitor is an interface where the computer communicates with you.

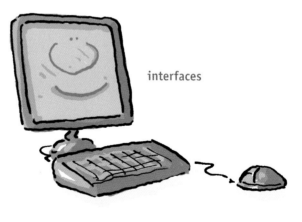 **keyboard p18 • mouse p19 monitor p19**

interfaces

initialize

To initialize a program is to start it up.

 **program p30**

menu

A menu is a choice of commands linked to a program that you are using. You get a menu of different commands when you right-click the mouse. There is also a strip called the menu bar at the top of a program window. When you click on a word in the menu, such as 'File' or 'Edit', you get a list of commands to choose from.

program p30

menu

mouseover

A mouseover is an area on a web page that changes when you move the pointer over it. It can be something very simple, such as a word changing its colour, or something more complicated such as an animation.

web page p47 • animated GIF p71

parallel port

A parallel port is one kind of connection on the back of a computer. It is used for connecting peripherals such as printers and scanners to the computer.

peripheral p20 • printer p21
scanner p21

path

The path is the unique 'address' of a file on a computer's hard drive. If you know a file's path, you can easily find it.

address p36

pixel

A pixel is one of the millions of tiny dots that make up a monitor screen. Combined together, the pixels produce all the text, pictures, and movies that you see on your monitor.

monitor p19

port

In computing, a port is a connection point where information passes in to and out of a computer.

port

plug-in

A plug-in is a piece of software that adds an extra feature to a program.

 menu p56 • program p30
software p26

pull-down menu

A pull-down menu, or drop-down menu, is a list of choices that appear when you click on part of a menu bar.

pull-down menu

QWERTY

QWERTY is the name for the layout of most computer keyboards. It is called this because the letters at the top left of the keyboard spell QWERTY.

keyboard p18

QUERTY keyboard

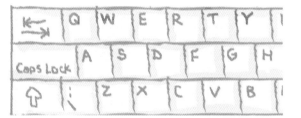

README file

A README file is the file that accompanies program files. It contains crucial instructions connected to the installation of a program.

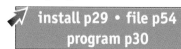 install p29 • file p54
program p30

read-only file

A read-only file is a file that can be opened and looked at, but cannot be altered.

file p54

reboot

To reboot means to restart a computer.

boot p51

screensaver

A screensaver is a moving image that comes up on the monitor screen when the computer has been idle for a certain period of time. It was originally used to protect a screen from being damaged. Nowadays, a screensaver has no purpose except to be entertaining.

monitor p19

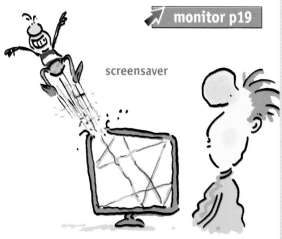

screensaver

scroll

To scroll is to move up or down through a document or file. Scroll-bars are bars that appear at the bottom and on the side of a window when a document is too big to fit on the screen. Clicking in the scroll-bar allows you to move up, down, to the left, or to the right in the document.

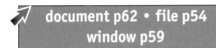
document p62 • file p54 window p59

shift key

The shift key is the one that is used to change from small letters (lower case) to capitals (upper case).

shortcut

A shortcut is an icon that takes you directly to a file or folder, or opens a program on your computer.

icon p74 • file p54 • folder p56

spacebar

The spacebar is the long bar at the front of a keyboard. When it is pressed it creates a space between words.

start menu

The start menu is the menu at the bottom left on a Windows PC. You can use it to start up a program, to open the control panel, or to shut down.

control panel p52 Windows® p31

startup folder

The startup folder contains shortcuts to all the programs that automatically start when you turn your computer on.

folder p54 • shortcut p58

subfolder

A subfolder is a folder inside another folder.

folder p54

task manager

The task manager is a box that lists all the processes running on a computer at a particular time. It can be used to shut down a program that has stopped working.

taskbar

The taskbar is a bar that usually runs along the bottom of a computer screen. It shows the start bar, shortcuts to regularly used programs and the icons of programs that are open.

icon p74 • program p30 shortcut p58 • start menu p58

template

A template is a set of rules for a document that can be used as a model for other documents. For instance, a template for writing letters has your name and address on it.

title bar

The title bar is the bar running across the top of an open window. It contains the name of the file as well as the controls for resizing it.

 file p54

toolbar

A toolbar has buttons for frequently used commands in a program.

 **command p67**

USB (universal serial bus)

A USB cable is a computer connection that transmits data very quickly.

user interface

The user interface is the place where the user can see or hear the information that a computer is producing. Usually this is the monitor screen. However, when the computer's output is sound the speakers are also a user interface.

 **graphical user interface p73**

warm boot

When you warm boot your computer, you restart it without turning off the power.

warm boot

wildcard

A wildcard is a character, usually an asterisk (*), that you use to stand for any letter or number when you are using a search engine. For instance, you could search for '*atherine' if you were not sure if someone's name was spelled Katherine or Catherine.

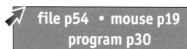 **search engine p45**

window

A window is the box that a file or program appears in when you open it. Different programs or files can be opened in different windows at the same time. You use the taskbar at the bottom of the screen to bring the one you want to work on to the top. This is the active window.

file p54 • mouse p19 program p30

zip files

Zip files are files that have been compressed using WinZip or a similar program. To look at a zipped file you need to 'unzip' it (expand it to its original size).

compress p51 program p30 • WinZip p31

Using a computer

Word processing

You have probably used your computer to write things. You might use a computer to write your work. If you do, you will do it using a word processing program. If want to make something like a leaflet or a booklet, with a combination of words and pictures, you might use a desktop publishing (DTP) program. But do you know about serif and sans serif fonts? What about headers and footers? Do you know how to format text and to set up style sheets? You can find out all about these things in this section.

copy and pasting is easy on a computer

access

To access something on the computer is to be allowed into a program, a file, or a web page. Sometimes you might have read-only access to a file. This means you can read it but you cannot change it or delete it. You need a password to access some programs or pages.

 **program p30 • file p54 web page p47**

align

Aligning is the process of making lines of type in a paragraph or page line up neatly one above the other.

This type is aligned left.

This type is aligned right.

Type is sometimes aligned on both sides, like this. This is called justified text. Each line is made the same length by making tiny adjustments to the size of the spaces between each word.

 **type p65**

antialiasing

Antialiasing is something a computer program does to the edges of letters to make them appear smooth. If you enlarge the letters on your computer screen, you will find they are made of millions of squares called pixels. This means the curves on, say, an 's' look all jagged. Antialiasing smoothes out these jagged edges to make the letters look sharp and clear.

 **pixel p56**

bold

Bold is a thicker kind of typeface (lettering). It is used to make words stand out, for instance in a heading. **These words are in bold type**.

 **type p65**

case

The case of a letter tells you what sort of letter it is. An upper case letter is a capital letter. Lower case means small letter.

case-sensitive

Case-sensitive words are usually passwords where you have to type the letters in the right case for the password to work. So if a case-sensitive password is 'paSSword', typing 'password' will not work.

 **password p85**

centre

To centre is a command used in word processing. If you centre a piece of text (writing) it sits in the middle of the page.

 **command p67 • text p64**

character

A character is any letter, number, or symbol that you can type with a keyboard.

keyboard p18

copy and paste

To copy and paste is one of the most useful functions on a computer. By pressing certain keys you can make exact copies of words or pictures. You can then paste the words or pictures somewhere else.

function keys p68

copy and paste

cut

To cut is to remove a picture or words from a file you are working on. The cut information is stored on the clipboard. This means that it can be pasted somewhere else in the file, or even in another program.

copy and paste p62
clipboard p51

desktop publishing (DTP)

Desktop publishing programs can be used to produce professional looking leaflets or books on your computer. Using a DTP program you can put together pictures and text to make the pages of a book or leaflet.

document

A document is usually a file with words (or words and pictures) that you can edit or change if you want to.

file p54

field

In a database, a field is a space that holds one piece of information.

font

A font is an alphabet of letters designed in a particular style. The two main types of fonts are called serif and sans serif.

F
A serif font. Serifs are the extra bits that stick out at the corners.

F
A sans serif font has no serifs.

Arial   Comic Sans

Times   **Snap**

Gill Sans   **Impact**

Goudy   Papyrus

COPPERPLATE

Eurostyle

 (Webdings)

a few different fonts

footer

The footer is the area at the bottom of the page in a written document. The page numbers often go here. The information in the footer appears on every page in the document.

 header p63

format

To format a document means to design it so that it looks the way you want. Changing the font used for text, or changing the colours or the way that text appears on the page, are all ways of altering the format.

Another meaning for format is to make a disk ready to store information. Floppy disks, CDs, and DVDs usually need to be formatted before you can store information on them.

 CD p16 • document p62
DVD p17 • floppy disk p17

header

The header is the area at the top of the page in a written document. The information in the header appears on every page of the document.

 footer p63

highlight

To highlight a word or section of text means to make it stand out by putting a colour behind it.

indent

Indents are used in word processing. Indenting a line of text means to start it further in from the edge. The first line of a new paragraph is often indented.

mail merge

Mail merge is a feature found in a word processing program. It automatically produces copies of the same letter, each with different address details.

mailing list

A mailing list is a list of email addresses to which the same message is automatically sent.

 email p39

OCR (optical character recognition)

An OCR program can recognise words typed on paper. It turns the written words into a digital document that can be edited on a computer.

↗ **digital p10**

OCR

RTF (rich text format)

Rich text format is a way of converting a word processing document into a form that can be shared with other programs.

spellchecker

The spellchecker is a function that you get in a word processing program. It checks the spelling of the words you type. There is also often a grammar checker, which checks that the sentences you write are correct English.

↗ **word processing p65**

sans serif font

Sans serif fonts are type fonts that have no serifs (the small 'curls' at the top and bottom of each letter). Arial and Helvetica are two well-known sans serif fonts.

E

a sans serif font

serif font

A serif font is a kind of type that has small 'curls' at the top and bottom of each letter. These curls are known as serifs. Times and Garamond are the names of two common serif fonts.

E

a serif font

style sheet

A style sheet is a set of instructions used by a word processing program to lay out a document consistently. It contains information such as the margins on the page, what is written in the headers and footers, and the styles of text used in the document.

text

Text means the words in a page or a document. Many kinds of document have a combination of text and graphics in them.

↗ **document p62 • graphics p73**

type

Type is another word for printed letters. A typeface is the look or style of a particular kind of lettering. There are many different typefaces. They are divided into two main kinds, serif and sans serif.

serif fonts

ABCDEFG
ABCDEFG
1234567890

ABCDEFG
abcdefg
1234567890

ABCDEFG
ABCDEFG
1234567890

ABCDEFG
abcdefg
1234567890

𝒜ℬ𝒞𝒟ℰℱ𝒢
abcdefg
1234567890

ABCDEFG
abcdefg
1234567890

sans serif fonts

ABCDEFG
abcdefg
1234567890

ABCDEFG
abcdefg
1234567890

ABCDEFG
abcdefg
1234567890

ABCDEFG
abcdefg
1234567890

ABCDEFG
abcdefg
1234567890

ABCDEFG
abcdefg
1234567890

sans serif p64 • serif font p64

word processing

Word processing means working with text on a computer. The first word processing programs were simple. They were designed so that you could use your computer as a typewriter. With a modern word processing program you can do much more. It has a range of different fonts, so you can use many different *kinds* **of lettering**. You can change the SIZE of the letters, or their colour. You can put them on a coloured background, or on a textured background. You can draw simple shapes like this △. You can even put pictures into a document. Word processing programs are used for writing anything from a letter or an email to a book.

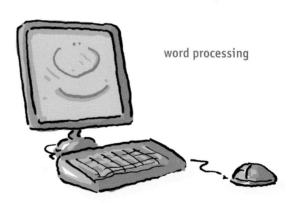

word processing

Commands

You might not think that you give your computer commands. But almost everything you do on the computer is a command of some kind. When you press a letter key you are telling the computer to show that letter on the screen. If you press the delete key you are commanding the computer to get rid of something. This section includes many of the commands that you use on the computer every day. There are also a few very simple command words that computer programmers might use, such as AND and OR.

using the 'undo' command

abort

To abort a program means to end it suddenly. You usually have to do this when the program is not working properly. If you abort a program you might lose the work you were doing. This is why it makes sense to save your work regularly.

➤ **program p30 • save p69**

AND

You can use AND when you search a database to look for something using more than one word. So a search for 'black AND cat' will find anything about black cats in the database. You don't need to put in the word 'AND' in most internet search engines.

➤ **database p80**

clear

To clear is a command that means the same as delete.

➤ **delete p67**

click

A click is the action performed with the buttons on a mouse. Usually, one click gives a command, two clicks opens a program, and a click with the right-hand mouse button opens up menus.

➤ **mouse p19 • menu p56 program p30**

command

A command is any instruction you give to your computer. For instance, print, delete, and save are all commands.

delete

To delete something is to get rid of it from the computer.

double-click

Double-clicking is a way of opening a file or a folder. You click twice with the left mouse button while the mouse pointer is hovering over the file or folder you want to open.

➤ **file p54 • folder p54 • cursor p52**

edit

To edit means to change or correct something. For instance, you could edit the text in a document, or the instructions in a computer program.

enter

This is a big key on the right-hand side of the keyboard. It usually says 'Enter' and has an arrow on it. You press the enter key when you want to say 'yes' to doing something. In a document, the enter key adds a line. For instance you might be given the choice of saving or deleting a picture in which case you would press 'enter' to confirm that you want to save it.

➤ **document p62 • keyboard p18**

find and replace

Find and replace is a command you find in most word processing programs. You can use the find command to find words or letters in a document. You can then use the replace command to replace those words or letters with something else.

function keys

Function keys are the keys along the top of your keyboard numbered F1 to F12. What makes them different from the other keys is that you can program each one to do a particular job. For instance, pressing F7 could turn any highlighted words green and bold.

**bold p61 • highlight p63
keyboard p18 • program p30**

insert

When you insert something on a computer, you add something. You might insert a picture into an essay, or insert a word into a sentence.

keyboard shortcuts

Keyboard shortcuts are ways that you can give the computer commands by pressing combinations of keys on the keyboard. This is much quicker than using the mouse and menus.

These shortcuts use the 'control' key at the lower left of the keyboard.

Ctrl + S	*save*
Ctrl + C	*copy*
Ctrl + X	*cut*
Ctrl + V	*paste*
Ctrl + L	*align text left*
Ctrl + R	*align text right*
Ctrl + E	*centre text*

menu p56 • mouse p19

load

When you load a program on to a computer you put it into the memory or on the hard disk drive.

hard disk p18 • memory p19

log on

Logging on is what you do to access the Internet. It usually means typing in a password and username. If your computer is part of a network, you may have to log on when you want to use the computer.

password p85 • username p46

log off

Logging off is the opposite of logging on. You log off when you leave the Internet, or a secure website. You may also log off from your computer if you are on a computer network.

network p44

Commands

move

Move is a command that you can use in Windows when you want to move a file from one place to another.

 Windows p31

OR

OR is a command you can use when you are using a search engine to look for something on the Internet. It will find websites with either of two words. For instance, if you search for 'Sun OR Moon', the search engine will find web pages with that have the word Sun or the word Moon in them.

 search engine p45

paste

Paste is a command that you use with copy. After you have copied something to the clipboard, you can put it somewhere else using the paste command. You can paste the thing you have copied somewhere else in the same document, or you can paste it into another document. You may be able to paste it into a completely different program.

 copy and paste p62
document p62

repeat

To repeat is an instruction to the computer to do something again and again.

return key

The return key on a keyboard is the one that instructs the computer to carry out a particular command such as open, save, and shut down. It is the same key as the enter key.

 enter p67

save/save as

Save is the command used to save data to the hard disk for future use. The 'Save as' command saves the file with a different name.

search

To search is to look for information on the Internet.

select

To select something is to highlight a particular word or object that needs to be changed in some way.

sort

To sort is the process of organising information under different topics or rules.

undo

Undo is a command that lets you go back and correct a mistake.

using the 'undo' command

Graphics and multimedia

Graphics are photographs, drawings, graphs, or any other kind of picture. Multimedia can mean music, pictures, film, or a combination of all three. Most people have used a graphics program to draw a picture using a computer. You might have taken photographs with a digital camera and looked at them on the computer, or scanned in photos from a book or magazine. But do you know the difference between vector graphics and raster graphics? Can you tell an MPEG from an MP3? You can find out about all these in this section.

pie chart

airbrush

The airbrush is a tool found in painting programs. When you draw with it, it is like using a can of spray paint.

airbrush

animated GIF

An animation is a moving picture. An animated GIF is a type of file used to create small moving images.

GIF p73

bar chart

A bar chart is a graph that shows information as different-sized bars.

bar chart

brush tool

You can find the brush tool in all painting programs. You will find it in its simplest form in Microsoft Paint. Its advantage is that it gives you a much wider variety of line shapes than the pen tool.

program p30

bitmap image

A bitmap image is one way a computer can produce images on the screen. If you mega-enlarge a picture you will see that it is actually made up of millions and millions of different squares of colour. When you look at the picture at normal size, all these squares merge and trick your eye into seeing colours and shading.

GIF p73 • JPEG p74 • pixel p56

brush tool

Graphics and multimedia

burn

To burn something is to record information on a CD or DVD.

➹ CD p16 • DVD p17

buttons

Buttons are one way of showing files on your desktop or in a window. When you click on a button, it takes you to a particular file or opens a program.

CAD (computer-aided design)

CAD programs are graphics programs used for designing 3D objects such as cars, buildings, and bridges.

➹ graphics p73 • program p30

chart

A chart is a way of visually displaying information.

clip art

Clip art is the name for collections of small pictures that you can use to brighten up your writing.

clip art

CMYK

CMYK stands for cyan (blue-green), magenta (pinkish red), yellow (yellow), and key (black). These four colours are the inks used in colour printers. A CMYK picture is one that is set up to look best when it is printed. RGB (red, green, blue) pictures are set up to look best on the computer screen.

➹ RGB p76

DAT (digital audio tape)

DAT is a type of magnetic tape that can hold large amounts of data. DAT tapes can be used to back up information on a computer.

➹ backing up p50

digital camera

A digital camera is a camera that can take pictures and short movies. Instead of storing the pictures on film, the camera stores the pictures digitally, as a computer does. You can look at the pictures or print them out from your computer, or you can take them to a photo lab and get high-quality prints made.

➹ digital p10

dpi (dots per inch)

This is the number of dots of ink that an inkjet printer puts on every inch of a page when printing a picture or words. The higher the dpi the better a picture will look.

A picture printed at 300 dpi will look better than if it is printed at 72 dpi.

inkjet printer p18

72 dpi   300 dpi

GIF

A GIF is a type of picture file. GIF pictures are usually small files. They are often used on web pages, because small pictures load quickly.

web page p47

grabber hand

The grabber hand is a hand-shaped icon. It is a tool found in some computer programs that lets you move an object on the screen when you click on it.

icon p74 • program p30

graph

A graph is a way of showing information on a chart or diagram.

graphical user interface (GUI)

Graphical user interface is a long name for something very simple. It means everything on your screen that makes it easy to use. The buttons, wallpaper, icons, menus, and symbols all make a computer much friendlier. Without it you would be faced with a black screen covered with strings of letters and numbers.

button p72 • icon p74
wallpaper p78

graphics

Graphics are pictures. A photo is a graphic and so is a diagram, a graph, or an icon. There are all kinds of programs for creating and looking at graphics on a computer. There are two main kinds of graphics files. Raster graphics, or bitmaps, are pictures made up of lots of tiny coloured dots called pixels. Photos and images that you can scan into the computer are raster graphics. Vector graphics are made up of combinations of lines, curves, and other shapes. They are not made of dots, so you can enlarge or reduce them without affecting their quality.

graph p73 • icon p74
pixel p56 • raster graphics p76
vector graphics p77

graphics accelerator

A graphics accelerator is used in computers to improve the performance of gaming. It contains its own specialised processor.

 processor p21

greyscale

A greyscale image is a black and white picture or photo.

halftone

A halftone picture is one that is made up of millions of tiny dots. The dots are different sizes and colours. When we look at the picture, our eyes blur the dots together and we see a picture. Printed photographs are made up of halftone dots.

handles

Handles are the little square boxes that you see around the edges of a picture when you place it in a document. They allow you to change its size.

 **document p62**

icon

Icons are small, simple pictures or symbols. Your desktop has many icons that take you straight to particular programs, folders, or files.

 **desktop p53**

image

An image is any picture or photograph.

jaggies

Jaggies are the zigzag edges that you get along the edges of bitmap images.

 **bitmap image p71**

JPEG

A JPEG is a type of picture file that has been compressed or made smaller than its original size. This is useful if you want to send pictures or drawings over the Internet, because pictures are often very big files. The trouble with JPEGs is that they make the file smaller by throwing away some of the information. The smaller you make a JPEG file, the worse the picture quality gets.

 **compress p51**

layer

Layers can be found in some drawing programs. They are a bit like pieces of transparent paper that you can move about or draw on individually. For instance you can draw most of a donkey on one layer and try out different-sized ears on another layer.

line graph

A graph is a way of showing information on a chart or diagram. In a line graph, the points on the graph are joined up by a line.

 bar chart p71 • pie chart p76

MIDI (musical instrument digital interface)

MIDI is a 'language' that allows electronic instruments to communicate with computers. MIDI devices can be used for making, recording, and playing back music.

MP3

MP3 files are sound or music files that are used a lot on computers and on the Internet. In an MP3 file the music is compressed, so that it takes up less space on the computer. However, the music still sounds as good as it would on a CD.

 **compress p51**

MP3 files

MPEG

An MPEG is a kind of file used for videos on the Internet and on computers. The MPEG is a way of compressing the video so that it takes up less space.

multimedia

A multimedia file on a computer is one that has a combination of words, sound or music, and pictures or video.

object

An object is anything that you can select with the cursor that can be changed or modified. Photos, graphs, and tables are all kinds of object.

 mouse p19 • cursor p52

palette

A palette is a range of colours. A monitor has a palette of colours that it is able to display.

pencil tool

There is a pencil tool in most graphics and printing programs. You can use it to draw lines.

pictogram

A pictogram conveys an idea by means of a simple picture rather than through words.

pie chart

A pie chart is a chart where the information is shown as 'slices' of a circular 'pie'.

pie chart

radio button

A radio button is a small circle next to each item in a list of choices. To choose an item in the list, you click on the radio button next to your choice.

○ DON'T KNOW

○ DON'T CARE

○ DON'T WANT

radio button

raster graphics

Raster graphics are bitmap images. These are pictures made up from tiny squares or pixels. Digital photographs or images that have been scanned into a computer are raster graphics. They are different from vector graphics. These are images drawn using lines, curves, and other kinds of shape.

 bitmap image p71 • pixel p56 vector graphics p77

resize

To resize, or rescale, an image means to change its size. You can do this by dragging one of the tiny 'handles' that appear at the corners or on the edges of an image when you click on it.

resolution

Resolution is the number of dots or pixels that make up an image. A high-resolution image has more pixels and is better quality than a low-resolution picture.

 **pixel p56**

RGB (red, green, blue)

Red, green, and blue are the three primary colours of light. Images for a computer look best if they are in RGB colour. This is because your monitor combines dots of these three colours to produce all the other colours you see on the screen.

 **CMYK p72**

rip (music)

To rip is to copy music from a CD on to your computer.

rip

rip (printer)

A rip is a device that converts computer data (information) into a form that can be understood by a printer.

spray tool

Spray tool is another name for the airbrush tool. It is used in painting and graphics programs.

↗ **airbrush p71**

texture

Texture describes the look and feel of different surfaces such as the soft texture of fur or the rough texture of sandpaper. Textured backgrounds look like textured substances.

vector graphics

Vector graphics are a way of drawing images on a computer. They are different from raster graphics, which break up an image into dots. Vector graphics use lines, curves, and other shapes to draw an image. They do not depend on resolution (the number of dots per inch) as a raster image does. This means that a vector image can be enlarged or reduced without losing quality.

↗ **raster graphics p76**
resolution p76 • dpi p73

texture

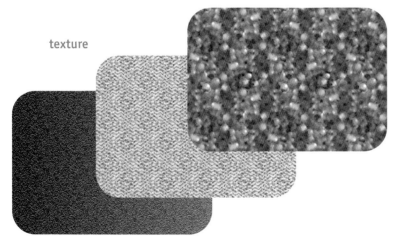

wallpaper

Wallpaper is the background colour or picture on the computer desktop. You can change the wallpaper to anything from a detailed photo to a plain white background.

wallpaper

WYSIWIG

WYSIWYG stands for 'What You See Is What You Get'. It means that what you see on the computer screen is exactly what will be on the page if you print the document out.

zoom

The zoom command makes an object or a document on the computer screen appear larger or smaller.

zoom

Data processing

Data is another word for imformation. A computer can handle all kinds of information, from numbers and sums to videos or sound files. If your data is to do with numbers, you might put it in a spreadsheet program. If you have a lot of data, and you want to be able to organise it in different ways, a database is the best kind of program to use. You can find out all about spreadsheets and databases in this section.

using a database program

access

To access something on the computer is be to allowed into a program or a file or web page. Sometimes you might have read-only access to a file. This means you can read it but you cannot change it or delete it. You need a special password to access some programs or pages.

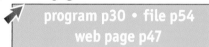
program p30 • file p54
web page p47

binary tree

A binary tree is a method of organising related data in a tree-like way. A common example of a binary tree is a diagram of a family tree.

data p80

branch

A branch is one part of a data tree.

cells

Cells are the boxes that make up a spreadsheet page. You can write numbers or formulae in cells.

spreadsheet p81

data

Data is another word for information.

data projector

A data projector projects data (information) on to a screen so that it can be seen by a group of people.

database

A database is a file of information. The information in a database may be about people (for instance, the customers of a company) or about things (for instance, the entries in an encyclopedia). You can search for information in a database in different ways. You can search a database for someone with a particular name, or for someone who lives at a certain address.

file p54

datalogging

Datalogging is using a computer and one or more sensors to collect and store information over a period of time. For instance, a computer connected to a temperature sensor can be used to record changes in temperature over several hours or days.

sensor p21

garbage in – garbage out

Garbage in – garbage out means that if you feed poor quality data into a computer you will get bad data out.

data p80

questionnaire

A questionnaire is a list of questions used to gather information about a particular topic.

spreadsheet

A spreadsheet is a program used to calculate by creating formulae. You can use it to draw up tables and charts. Each page of a spreadsheet is divided into many boxes (cells), each of which can hold a piece of information (for instance, a number or a piece of text).

cells p80 • formula p10 program p30

spreadsheet

Computer security

Computer security is about keeping the files and data on your computer safe from damage, and stopping people from sending you data you don't want. You have probably heard of hackers, who try to get into other people's computers. But have you heard of samurai? We all know about computer viruses that can destroy files on your computer or even stop it working altogether. But what about Trojan horses or mandelbugs? You probably know about spam, which is unwanted email. But do you know about mailbombs, or leapfrog attacks?

hacking into a computer

antivirus software

Antivirus software is a program that protects your computer from viruses and gets rid of any that are already there.

program p30 • virus p86

antivirus software

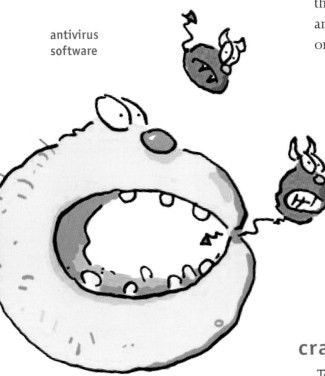

bug

A bug is the name for an error in a computer program that stops it from working properly. There is a story that, way back in ancient computer history, an insect got into a computer. It blew out some electronic circuits, and made the machine burn out. After that, anything that went wrong was blamed on 'a bug'. Believe it or believe it not!

program p30

authenticate

Authenticate means to check that something is genuine or correct. For instance, if you type in an email address, your email server will check to make sure the address is a real one.

address p36 • email p39 server p22

crack

To crack is to illegally break into a computer without the owner's permission.

cracker

A cracker is someone who tries to break through the security system on a computer. Usually they do this to steal information.

Computer security

encode/encrypt

To encode or encrypt something means to put it into a code that cannot be read by other people. Personal information held on the Internet, such as people's bank details, is encoded to stop other people from reading it.

encode/encrypt

> Internet p33

firewall

A firewall is a type of security program that prevents unwanted people or programs from using the Internet to get on to your computer.

> program p30

hacker

A hacker is someone who looks for weaknesses in computer programs and tries to disrupt them. This can cause serious problems if the program runs vital things such as air traffic control. Hackers also use the Internet to try to break into the computer systems of governments or big companies. Some hackers do this to steal money or to cause trouble. Other hackers just do it to show that they can.

> program p30

junk mail

Junk mail is the unpleasant or unwanted email that people get in their inbox from time to time. Another name for junk mail is spam.

> email p39 • spam p86

leapfrog attack

A leapfrog attack occurs when someone illegally uses a password to get into a website. They then use the information they steal to break into lots more sites. For instance, getting hold of a bank's password might make it possible for a crook to get into the bank accounts of many customers.

leapfrog attack

> password p85 • website p47

hacker

letterbomb

A letterbomb is an email that contains a virus.

letterbomb

email p39
virus p86

mailbomb

To mailbomb is to flood an email address with mail.

mandelbug

A mandelbug is a type of complex computer bug.

bug p83

monitoring

Computers are often used for monitoring. This means continuously collecting information and checking it. When a computer monitors something (for example the engines of an airliner) it can spot something wrong before it becomes dangerous.

monitoring

password

A password is a word or phrase that only you know, that protects a part of the computer, or your emails. You may need a password to get on to your computer or on to the Internet. You can also protect files that you want to keep private with a password.

email p39

password

samurai

A samurai is a type of hacker who is hired to perform legal hacking, such as helping the police get information from a criminal's computer.

samurai

hacker p84

Computer security

security

Security programs protect your computer and files from viruses and other kinds of damage. Often these get on to your computer from the Internet. There are two kinds, anti-virus programs and firewall programs.

> **antivirus software p83**
> **firewall p84 • program p30**
> **virus p86**

security

spam

Spam is unwanted email, sometimes quite unpleasant, which is sent out through the Internet. Computer viruses are often spread through spam emails.

> **email p39 • virus p86**

spam

Trojan horse

A Trojan horse is a computer virus that arrives over the Internet disguised as friendly email.

Trojan horse

virus

A virus is a small piece of computer code that is designed to harm a computer. The virus makes copies of itself and puts them in the programs and documents on your computer. Sometimes the virus changes as it copies itself, making it harder to find. If your computer gets a bad virus, it can spoil all your files and destroy your programs.

> **document p62 • file p54**
> **program p30**

virus

worm

Worm is another name for an Internet worm.

> **Internet worm p42**

Computer jargon

This section is about jargon - special words used by computer people. A few words, such as geek and FAQ, have become part of the language. However, many of the words in this section are silly words that are used for fun. The Internet is sometimes called cyberspace - but have you heard of cyber-squatting or cyberbunnies? You may have heard of plug and play - but what about plug and pray? In this section you can find out about everything from goat files and fish queues to fungus and asbestos underpants.

number crunching

adger

If you adger something you ruin a document or computer by doing something absolutely stupid. For instance, knocking a can of cola all over your computer would probably adger the machine.

adger

AFK

AFK is an abbreviation for Away From Keyboard.

√ keyboard p18

all elbows

A program that is all elbows is one that takes up most of the computer's power and elbows other programs out of the way. This often causes the computer to freeze up.

√ program p30

alpha geek

An alpha geek is the genius that other geniuses go to for advice. It would definitely not be cool to be seen out with them.

ambimousterous

Ambimousterous is having the skill to use a computer mouse with either hand.

√ mouse p19

annoyware

Annoyware is a computer program that you are allowed to try out, but then it keeps on nagging you to pay for it.

√ program p30

annoyware

asbestos underpants

Asbestos underpants are the imaginary underwear you put on while you wait for the reply to a rude or insulting email. For example, 'I'm expecting, a good telling off after that cheeky email I sent so I've put on my asbestos underpants.'

asbestos underpants

√ email p39

ambimousterous

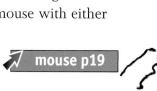

Computer jargon

banana problem

A banana problem is the sort of problem that goes on and on with no solution in sight. The name supposedly comes from the story of a child who said 'I know how to spell banana, but I don't know when to stop.'

banana problem

bells and whistles

Bells and whistles are fancy extras that sometimes come with a computer. They are supposed to make the computer more attractive, but in fact they are pretty useless. Who wants a computer that presses your trousers anyway?

bells and whistles

black hole

A black hole is the place that all those emails that never arrive disappear into.

email p39

blow away

To blow away files is to delete them from your computer by accident.

file p54

brain dump

To brain dump is to tell someone everything you know about a particular subject.

brain dump

breadcrumbs

Breadcrumbs is the name for any feature in an Internet program that lets you track where you have been. It works by highlighting or colouring links you have already visited. This saves you from visiting the same place twice by mistake.

Internet p33 • program p30

Computer Jargon

catatonic

A computer goes catatonic when it completely freezes and refuses to respond to any amount of arm-waving or shouting. For example, 'I was just finishing the essay when the computer decided to go catatonic. No matter how much I threatened it with my chair, I ended up having to shut the thing down and lost my all my hard work.'

catatonic

chug

When a computer begins to chug it starts to work slowly. This is usually because it is being asked to do too much.

coaster

A coaster is a useless CD – one that you have trodden on or that has been chewed by the dog.

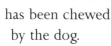

CD p16

coaster

computer jargon

Computer jargon is special computer words that are used by computer enthusiasts. Many of the words in this dictionary are computer jargon.

cough and die

Cough and die is what an old, outdated program does when it is unable to cope with what it is asked to do and probably crashes.

program p30

crash and burn

Crash and burn is an extra-spectacular crash.

crash p52

crash and burn

cyberbunny

A cyberbunny is someone who knows next to nothing about computers and tries to advise others about them.

cyber-squatting

Cyber-squatting is when someone registers the name of a famous company, such as Nike or Lego, as a domain name on the Internet. They then try to sell the domain name to the company for lots of money when they come to set up a website.

 **domain name p38 • website p47**

dancing frog

A dancing frog is the sort of computer problem that never happens when anyone else is looking.

dead tree

Dead tree is another term for paper. For example, you might say 'I read the article on the Internet while he insisted on reading the dead tree version'.

Internet p33

drone

A drone is the sort of brainless shop assistant in a computer store that refuses to leave you alone and drowns you in sales talk.

drunk mouse effect

The drunk mouse effect is when the cursor on the screen refuses to follow the movements of your mouse. Instead it moves about with a mind of its own.

cursor p52 • mouse p19

drunk mouse effect

examining the entrails

Examining the entrails is looking through the computer to try to find the cause of a fault.

examining the entrails

face time

Face time is time spent actually talking to someone face to face, rather than electronically via email.

📩 email p39

FAQ (frequently asked questions)

FAQs are the questions most often asked about a certain subject, such as problems with games or with using a certain type of printer. Manufacturers often post lists of FAQs on their websites.

📩 website p47

feature shock

Feature shock is what you get when you load 'Battle Star Obliterator' and find you are in charge of 28 armies with 45 different weapons and 86 kinds of missile. There are so many features, you become completely confused!

feature shock

fish queue

A fish queue is when the computer slows down and all the actions it is supposed to be carrying out start to back up one behind the other.

flame

If you flame someone on the Internet you give him or her a piece of your mind.

📩 Internet p33

flood fill

Flood fill is a way of filling a large area with colour when using a painting program. It is usually shown by a paint bucket symbol.

flood fill

fritterware

Fritterware is the sort of program that uses lots of computing power but doesn't do very much. Because it is very flashy you think it is worth having.

📩 program p30

gearhead

A gearhead is a person who always has to have the very latest gadget or game.

geek

A geek is the computer equivalent of a swot.

genius from Mars technique

To use the genius from Mars technique is to solve a difficult problem in a completely new and original way that no one else has thought of.

gnarly

Gnarly is used to describe any problem that is difficult to understand or to solve.

gnarly

flatline

When something goes flatline, it breaks down.

grok

To grok is to understand something to do with computing really clearly.

heatseeker

A heatseeker is someone buying computer equipment who always wants the latest version of software or other computer products, even when it doesn't really make much difference.

 software p24

hungry puppy

A hungry puppy is a program that only operates when the computer has nothing else to do.

program p30

hungry puppy

hungus

Something that is hungus is large and awkward. This could be a picture, a movie, or some other large file.

↗ file p54

hungus

kludge

A kludge is a way of referring to something that has been poorly designed or badly thought out.

kludge

leetspeak

This is a kind of slang used by computer hackers and other computer geeks. In leetspeak some of the letters in a word are replaced by numbers. For instance '13375p33k' means leetspeak.

↗ hacker p84 • geek p93

LOL

LOL is an abbreviation used in chat rooms. It stands for Lots Of Luck, or sometimes Laugh Out Loud or Lots Of Love.

↗ chat room p37

lurker

A lurker is a person who hangs around in the background of Internet chat rooms listening in on everyone else's conversation but not actually taking part themselves.

↗ chat room p37

lurker

meatspace

Meatspace is the 'real' world. It is the opposite of cyberspace – the world of computers.

mouse elbow

Mouse elbow is a pain in your arm caused by using a computer mouse too much.

↗ mouse p19

multitask

To multitask is to carry out several jobs at once. A computer that has a single processor can only do one thing at a time. However, it can do several different things one after the other so quickly that it seems like multitasking.

> ⬈ **processor p21**

multitask

nagware

Nagware is the kind of shareware that has a large screen at the beginning or end of the program reminding you to register the program.

> ⬈ **program p30 • shareware p31**

nailing jelly to a tree

This is another way of saying that something is almost impossible to do. For instance, trying to draw a picture with a mouse can be like nailing jelly to a tree.

> ⬈ **mouse p19**

netiquette

Netiquette is using considerate behaviour when taking part in Internet chat rooms.

> ⬈ **chat room p37**

nude

A computer that is nude is one that does not have an operating system.

> ⬈ **operating system p30**

number crunching

Number crunching means doing a large number of calculations.

nailing jelly to a tree

off the trolley

If a program is not working properly, it is off the trolley.

↗ **program p30**

off the trolley

one-banana problem

A one-banana problem is one that is simple to solve.

plug and pray

Plug and pray is when something is supposed to work straight away, but it doesn't.

power hit

A power hit is a sudden change in the power supply to a computer. Power hits are often the result of electrical storms, they can cause crashes and even permanent damage to your computer.

↗ **crash p52**

propellerhead

A propellerhead is another term for a swot or geek.

↗ **geek p93**

propellerhead

raster burn

Raster burn is eyestrain brought about by too many hours spent looking at a monitor that is out of focus.

↗ **monitor p19**

power hit

return from the dead

To return from the dead is to start using the Internet after a long absence.

▸ **Internet p33**

return from the dead

ROFL (rolling on the floor laughing)

ROFL is Internet jargon for laughter.

snailmail

Snailmail is the old-fashioned letter post, rather than email.

▸ **email p39**

snailmail

snarf

To snarf is to copy a document or file and use it without the author's permission.

▸ **document p62 • file p54**

spider food

Many websites have long lists of words hidden in their pages so that they will be picked up by search engines. These lists of words are called spider food.

▸ **website p47 • search engine p45**

spider food

tired iron

A tired iron is a computer or hardware that is old but still works perfectly well.

▸ **hardware p13**

tired iron

Computer Jargon

toaster

A toaster is old-fashioned or slow hardware.

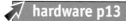
hardware p13

turbo nerd

A turbo nerd is a nerd with bells on.

wave a dead chicken

To wave a dead chicken over something is to hope a problem will sort itself out.

wave a dead chicken

wetware

Wetware is the people involved with a computer system: programmers, administrators, and computer operators. When you are working on a computer, you are a piece of wetware!

zipperhead

A zipperhead is a person with a closed mind.

zipperhead

YMMV (your mileage may vary)

YMMV is Internet slang, meaning that something may work in one way for one person, but it may work very differently for another.

Internet p33

your mileage may vary

This last section includes all the words that are not covered in the other sections of the book. Here you will find entries for some important computer companies, such as Microsoft and Intel. There are also entries about the people who use computers - the end users. Keywords and smileys, downtime, and simulation - you can find out about all these words in this section.

computer simulation

AI

AI stands for artificial intelligence. Most computers make the same mistake over and over again. They can't learn from their mistakes. But computers with AI are actually able to learn simple things, such as how to read handwriting. Scientists predict that computers will gradually become more and more intelligent. Who knows? Maybe one day a PC with AI will be Prime Minister!

PC p20

AI

buffer

A buffer allows you to listen to music or watch a video on the Internet without any pauses or hiccups. The computer loads up a bit of the music or video before it starts playing. This is the buffer. Then if your Internet connection slows down or stops for a second or two, the computer can play the buffer to fill the gap.

Internet p33

disable

To disable a program is to temporarily stop it working.

program p30

downtime

Downtime is any time when a computer is shut down because it is not working properly.

downtime

dump

To dump is to quickly transfer information from a computer to a printer. Technicians do this when they are looking at data to sort out a problem.

data p80

dump

emoticon

An emoticon is a simple way of showing emotions in an email using the keys of your keyboard. If you look at emoticons sideways they look like faces.

:-)	**:-v**
happy	*shouting*
:-(	**:-x**
sad	*a kiss*

email p39 • keyboard p18

emulator

An emulator is a piece of computer hardware, such as a printer, that can run on software designed for another machine.

hardware p 13 • printer p20
software p24

end user

The end user is the person who actually uses a computer program after it has been developed and tested.

program p30

Intel

Intel is a large company that makes microprocessors – the 'brains' inside every computer.

microprocessor p19

interactive

An interactive program is one in which the person using it has to answer questions or do things. Computer games and educational programs are good examples of interactive programs.

program p30

interactive whiteboard

An interactive whiteboard is the electronic equivalent of a blackboard.

interactive whiteboard

keywords

Keywords are the words used by a search engine to find web pages on the Internet. If you type in a keyword or words, the search engine will link to all the web pages containing those words.

search engine p45
Internet p33
web page p47

Other terms

Microsoft®

Microsoft® is the company that developed Windows®, the world's most successful computer operating system.

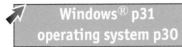

Windows® p31
operating system p30

priority

Priority is the relative importance given to different processes by a computer. If a computer is very busy the CPU will decide to do the most important tasks first. Other processes will dramatically slow down, or stop, until the job that has been given priority is complete.

CPU p10

public domain

Being in the public domain means that any information, such as software, may be freely used by everyone.

software p24

query

A query is a question, for instance something you might ask a search engine.

search engine p45

queue

A queue is the list of documents waiting to be printed.

document p62

sequence

A sequence is a group of computer commands that need to be carried out in a particular order.

simulation

A simulation is a computer model of a real-life event. Scientists use computer simulations in many different ways. For instance, they build complicated simulations of what is happening in the air to help make good weather forecasts.

simulation

smiley

A smiley is another word for an emoticon.

emoticon p101

user

The user is the person using a particular computer.

Index

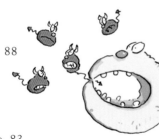

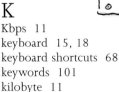

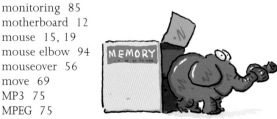

U

undo 69
uninstall 31
UNIX 31
upload 31
URL 46
USB 59
usenet 46
user 102
user interface 59
username 46

V

vapourware 31
vector graphics 77
virus 39, 86

W

wallpaper 78
WAP (wireless application protocol) 46
warm boot 59
wave a dead chicken 98
web 48
web page 47
web space 47
webcam 47
webmaster 46
website 47
wetware 98

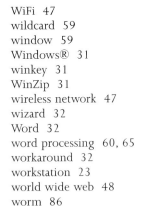

WiFi 47
wildcard 59
window 59
Windows® 31
winkey 31
WinZip 31
wireless network 47
wizard 32
Word 32
word processing 60, 65
workaround 32
workstation 23
world wide web 48
worm 86
WYSIWYG 78

X

XML 48

Y

YMMV (your mileage may vary) 98

Z

zip drive 23
zip files 59
zipperhead 98
zoom 78

Oxford subject dictionaries

Oxford ABC and 123 Picture Rhyme book
Oxford Picture Word Book

Oxford First Rhyming Dictionary
Oxford Junior Rhyming Dictionary

Oxford First Maths Dictionary
Oxford First Science Dictionary

Oxford Primary Maths Dictionary
Oxford Primary Science Dictionary

Oxford Mathematics Study Dictionary
Oxford Science Study Dictionary

Think dictionaries. Think Oxford